God Verses
The Bad Boy

God Verses The Bad Boy

▲ ▲ ▲

Marty McFly: "Wait a minute. Wait a minute, Johnny. Ah…are you telling me that you built a time machine… using a timeline?"

John Murray

ISBN: 1533337160
ISBN 13: 9781533337160

DEDICATION

▲ ▲ ▲

This book is dedicated to all those who have graduated from or are going through the reGROUP program at Summit Church in Orlando, Florida, along with those who have passed through or are part of Summit's campus in the Horizon Dorm at the 33rd Street Jail.

My sister Dorothy and lifetime friend Tommy G. They have been part of the Alcohol Anonymous program in the Bronx for over thirty-five years and are two of the most dedicated individuals I have ever known in my life. Having gone through the struggles and fears of alcoholism, they now lead others to sobriety.

Most of all, I dedicate this book to my family and friends who grew up in the Castle Hill housing projects. Without one or all of these groups, this book would not have been published.

ACKNOWLEDGMENT

▲ ▲ ▲

To my awesome, beautiful wife Marie who had to endure over thirty-five years of listening to my childhood stories but never tired of them or at least she never showed it! Because of her interest, I was able to keep them fresh in my mind.

A NOTE OF EXPLANATION
TO THE READER

▲ ▲ ▲

"VERSES" OR "VERSUS"? THAT IS THE QUESTION...

WHEN THIS BOOK WAS only a few short weeks away from publication, I suddenly realized that I needed to include an explanation of the title. Many people kept trying to correct my spelling of the word *verses*. Naturally, they thought the title was referencing some kind of boxing match between God and the bad boy. If that were the case, the title would need to be *God Versus the Bad Boy*. On the contrary, the title refers to the fact that God, in His ultimate mercy, showers the "bad boy" with wonderful inspiration-filled Bible verses. God quite literally "verses" this bad boy. In the eyes of God, there are no bad boys—only those unfortunate souls who harden their hearts against Him.

These stories are *not* meant to be an interpretation of Scripture; rather, they are personal reflections revealed to me by the Holy Spirit. When reading the verses that go along with the stories, I believe it is always wise to ask God to reveal to you through the Holy Spirit what they mean.

DISCLAIMER

▲ ▲ ▲

PSALM 88:12 (ESV) … "ARE your wonders known in the darkness or your righteousness in the land of forgetfulness?"

To the best of my recollection, every story in this book is true and involves the people, places, actions, and events described. But memory can play strange tricks at times, so if I have placed events out of sequence, attributed statements or behavior to the wrong person, or went beyond and stretched my imagination, I hereby heartily apologize. And of course, this admission, in no way rules out the wonderful awesome power and influence the Holy Spirit had in connecting the dots that pertains to my childhood story.

CONTENTS

WHAT'S HAPPENING?

▲ ▲ ▲

Acts 19:31 (NIV) … "Even some of the officials of the province, friends of Paul, sent him a message begging him not to venture into the theater."

God Verses the Bad Boy is an adventurous, humorous, heartwarming, sometimes heartbreaking collection of short, broken-up stories that send one kid back in time to his childhood mishaps in the Bronx Castle Hill projects. This "bad" boy's story is saturated with over 260 verses of Scripture that splash hope into his future.

Inspiration for this unexpected timeline comes from a musical production titled "The Prodigal Musical." The production was based on the prodigal son parable (Luke 15:11-32), produced by Summit Church, and performed at the Orlando Fringe Festival at Loch Haven Park during the spring of 2015.

One place in the musical captivated the audience when the younger bad boy brother named Dewey, after feeding the pigs for years, throws up his hands in disgust and says, "How did I get into this mess?" He then breaks into a song titled "Dad Will Be Mad." Throughout the song, Dewey gives the audience a timeline of his life. Interested parties can find the song track for "The Prodigal Musical" on iTunes.

1 Corinthians 2:7 (ESV) … *"But we impart a secret and hidden wisdom of God, which God decreed before the ages for our glory."*

If you picked up this book, hoping to get some answers for your own life, I can only point you to the road I took. As you continue to read the verses along with accompanying stories, ask the Holy Spirit to open your eyes for a connection. If you read this book only for the adventure, the humor, the heartwarming and the heartbreaking stories, you have missed the beauty of Scripture.

My prayer to God the Father is that He makes the Holy Spirit visible to all who read this book and that He will open their eyes, allowing them to see the deeper meaning of their own lives through these verses of Scripture.

Psalm 40:5 (NIV) … *"Many, LORD my God, are the wonders you have done, the things you planned for us. None can compare with you; were I to speak and tell of your deeds, they would be too many to declare."*

Have you ever wondered where God was when you were a child? Relax and drift back to those days full of excitement when you first discovered what this world was all about. Remember the lonely, scary nights falling asleep with your lamp still turned on? Whether you had a wonderful, mediocre, or terrible childhood, you can rest assured the Lord was watching over you.

Ecclesiastes 7:10 (NASB) … *"Do not say, 'Why is it that the former days were better than these?' For it is not from wisdom that you ask about this."*

When reflecting back on your childhood years, do you sometimes think life just did not turn out the way your childhood mind expected it to? If so, take heart that God, in His infinite wisdom, has been in control of your life the whole time. Jeremiah 1:5 (NIV) says, *"Before I formed you in the womb I knew you, before you were born I set you apart; I appointed you as a prophet to the nations."*

Isaiah 5:21 (NIV) … *"Woe to those who are wise in their own eyes and clever in their own sight."*

I am not a doctor, a therapist, a pastor, or a spiritual advisor; I'm just a kid from the Bronx who discovered God as an adult and then when looking back, I realized I had discovered Him in my childhood.

This book will evaluate specific moments throughout the first dozen or so years of my life that enlightened me as to how God played an integral part in my story—even when I had no idea of His existence. Rather than rely upon worldly wisdom and life lessons from the streets of the Bronx, I will draw connections between Scripture verses and my story to portray how healing, justification, clarification, and understanding of a loving, merciful, and awesome God has and will always remain present in my life.

So the question you are likely to ask at the end of this book is, "Could there be a verse of Scripture for each event in my life?" I believe so, and 2 Timothy 3:16 (NIV) would be what led me to believe so, as *"All Scripture is God-breathed and is useful for teaching, rebuking, correcting and training in righteousness."*

Writing this book was a trip back in time. The roller coaster ride of emotions was amusing, though sometimes painful, but always ripe with memories of those people and places that touched my life! Only as I grew older did I begin to realize some of the more in-depth meaning of some of these Bible verses.

THE BRONX

▲ ▲ ▲

1 CHRONICLES 6:54 (NIV) ... "These were the locations of their settlements allotted as their territory (they were assigned to the descendants of Aaron who were from the Kohathite clan, because the first lot was for them)."

I find it absolutely amazing that my place of birth in this wonderful world happened to be "The Bronx," a 57-square-mile borough famous for the spectacular Bronx Zoo, the birthplace of hip-hop music, and home of the New York Yankees. But when I landed here back in the 1950s, I was told it was a much simpler place than it is today. Though I was alive in the 1950s, I have no recollection of life. In that time, I existed solely for the enjoyment and entertainment of others.

Hebrews 11:1 (NIV) ... "Now faith is confidence in what we hope for and assurance about what we do not see."

If you have ever stopped to contemplate your existence, I imagine you asked a lot of the same questions as I did. Of all the places on the face of the earth, why did God place me here? Was I born with a specific mission for my life? Does God have a purpose or plan holding true with reason and without doubt? Did God create me with my physical features, race, and gender for a reason? Will God ever reveal the mystery of my life? As I meditate on the Bible verse at the start of this chapter and reflect back on where I have come in life, I lean toward answering all these questions with a resounding "YES!"

1 Corinthians 13:12 (NIV) ... "For now we see only a reflection as in a mirror; then we shall see face to face. Now I know in part; then I shall know fully, even as I am fully known."

But I'm getting ahead of myself. I should start at the very beginning because one thing I have learned through my journey thus far in life is you can't know how you got to where you are today without reflecting on the path you took to get you there. So now join me as I extract from the deepest parts of my inner being to what has now become the holiest memories I could have ever imagined in this lifetime.

MY EARLIEST MEMORY

▲ ▲ ▲

GENESIS 1:1 (KJV) … "IN the beginning God created the heavens and the earth."

Although we weren't present during the times when God created the universe, we have the book of Genesis to fill us in on the details. This is very much like life. While most don't remember their actual birth, we know it happened and have evidence to prove it occurred (photos, stories, and a birth certificate). My earliest memory of life, however, goes as far back as remembering the feeling of pressure and the tight squeeze as I was being pushed down, along with a slow motion sensation of being driven forward wrapped in a cocoon and drenched in complete darkness.

Now, I already know what you're thinking. "There is no way you could possibly remember this monumental event." But I do…I could hear only sounds of silence as I drifted into an abyss. Then suddenly, I felt what could only be described as a veil being lifted from my entire body. As my eyes opened, I saw a bright-white screen, and I heard voices all around me. The commotion and excitement was due to the fact that I had finally arrived…Yes!

There I was on the inside of an early 1960s station wagon, squashed tightly together with eight other uniquely created individuals who were all related to me by blood: my mom, my dad, my brothers, and my sisters. The experience I just described was at the Bronx Whitestone Drive-In Movie Theater. (What? Did you really think I remembered my own birth?!)

I was tucked tightly under a blanket with my siblings on the floor of our station wagon. We were hiding from the attendant who collected a fee for each passenger inside your car. As I tried to lift myself from under the blanket, my brothers and sisters pushed me back under and told me to be silent as the gentleman poked his head into our car for a headcount to charge the appropriate fee for entrance.

Matthew 11:15 (NLT) … "Anyone with ears to hear should listen and understand."

Before the flick started, I can recall and feel the breeze along with the tingling feeling of swinging back and forth on the swings in front of the gigantic intimidating white movie screen as my siblings squealed with laughter in the background.

While I cannot recall what double feature was playing that night, I foggily remember falling fast asleep right when the featured film started to play. I woke up briefly enough during intermission to get a glimpse of animated cartoon characters in the forms of hot dogs and ice cream Dixie cups, dancing on the huge screen and entertaining the patrons.

Once the movie ended and the car rolled back to our apartment, I can remember the sleepy comfort of being held in the arms of my sister Alice, as I was carried over her shoulder with my body dangling halfway down her back as she walked through ankle-deep, slimy mud. Then I was passed like a football into our first-floor kitchen apartment window, which was a much quicker route than having to walk into the building entrance and down our long hall-way. That one tiny memory was the first to start a building block known as my life.

THE CASTLE HILL PROJECTS

▲ ▲ ▲

JOHN 14:2 (KJV) … "IN my Father's house are many mansions: if it were not so, I would have told you. I go prepare a place for you."

The account of my life in this world begins as I am assigned into a large Irish Catholic family. The members of this clan (in descending age order) comprise of Alice, Michael, Tommy, Dorothy, Billy, Johnny, Jimmy and Peggy, Mom (Mary) and Dad (Michael). We dwelled in a twelve-story apartment building still under massive construction as a part of the Castle Hill projects located in the northeast section of the Bronx.

Our building sprouted out three great wings: one towards Castle Hill Avenue, one in the direction of Seward Avenue, and the third facing the twenty-story building. Every hallway had four apartments on each wing per floor. There were approximatley144 apartments in our building numbered 2160, where my family resided.

We were the original occupants of Apartment 1-B, complete with its fresh smelling coat of paint and brand new appliances, cabinets, and tiles throughout. The trees, shrubs and grass being planted contributed to my sensations of everything being new, along with my life. Smack dab across from us was building 2140, and between these two buildings stood the community's playground with wood benches, iron monkey bars, a seesaw, and a fountain that jolted water high into the air cooling off overheated children on those hot, steamy summer days. God graciously designated me to live in that building for the next fifteen years.

1 Kings 6:7 (NKJV)… "And the temple, when it was being built, was built with stone finished at the quarry, so that no hammer or chisel or any iron tool was heard in the temple while it was being built."

Territory-wise, if you stood on the corner of Castle Hill and Seward Avenues looking straight down Castle Hill Avenue toward the East River, on your right you would see building 635 towering directly over Castle Hill Avenue. In addition to having an awesome Castle Hill address, building 635 was superior in that it had 20 stories (not like the 12 stories where I lived). Those elevators traveled up and down at more extreme speeds than our elevators. All together the Castle Hill projects, which had eleven buildings with twelve stories and three buildings with twenty stories, was home for thousands of adults and children living within a four city block area. God had placed me smack into the center of constant activity with an electrifying atmosphere.

Each twelve-story building had two elevators; one elevator stopped on the odd-numbered floors, and the other stopped on the even-numbered floors. The twenty-story buildings also had two elevators, and both would stop on each floor. Our family had no need for an elevator because we lived on the first floor, but that didn't stop us from ascending and descending several times a day as we rode up and down in those shiny, humming boxes for the sole purpose of our own amusement!

Above photo: early 1960s era, in the far distance is unfinished
building, 2160 Seward Avenue. To the right is building 635 Castle
Hill Avenue also unfinished. Not seen in the photo is unfinished
building 2140 Seward Avenue, which is to the left of building 2160.

Luke 8:17 (NIV) ... *"For there is nothing hidden that will not be disclosed,
and nothing concealed that will not be known or brought out into the open."*

As a juvenile, my imagination would run wild, and I would pretend
that our building lobby was anything from a spaceship to a sinking
submarine. It had two gigantic, decorative, cement columns, which I
thought at the time held up the entire building. I certainly got a kick
out of running and hiding behind these gigantic columns, pretending at times I was invisible.

One day during a cold, stormy February day, when I was enjoying my favorite activity, the side entrance doors to the building flew
open, and in scurried a sopping-wet middle-aged woman. She was
struggling with her umbrella, which the wind had just turned inside

out, and at the same time, she was trying to balance herself on the wet, slippery lobby floor. Walking right behind her was a gentleman in a trench coat and hat, who was also soaked from the recent downpour. Together they stood there like two dogs shaking off the cold, wet rain from their bodies.

After a few minutes, the woman spotted me hiding behind the columns in my favorite spot, and I knew instantly I was no longer invisible to the outside world. She called out in a loud, commanding voice that echoed throughout the entire lobby, "YOU MUST BE JOHNNY!!"

As she moved swiftly in my direction, panic overwhelmed me, and I ran as fast as I could to escape this strange woman. I ran around and around the gigantic columns while she was in hot pursuit slipping and sliding right behind me. She was running as quick as she could, trying to grab hold of the back of my jacket. I ran from column to column trying to dodge her grasp until she cleverly changed directions, and I slammed smack into her awaiting arms as she yelled, "GOTCHA!" She then tossed me to the gentleman who, in turn, hoisted me high up toward the sky and onto his shoulders, carrying me off toward my apartment.

Ezekiel 19:4 (NASB) … "Then nations heard about him; He was captured in their pit, And they brought him with hooks To the land of Egypt."

"Who is this strange woman?" I thought as my heart was beating and beating at a frightening pace. I didn't know this strange woman accompanied by a doubly strange-looking man who had just jolted me high into the air. I struggled, tugging to get away from him. After a minute, I managed to slip both my arms out from my jacket.

Then clawing myself away, I hurled from his arms, tumbled to the floor, leaving my jacket hanging over his shoulder and halfway down his chest. I took off running full speed down the hall to our apartment, scurrying straight into our back bedroom. Then I slid right under my bed, panting and sweating as I listened bewildered to what sounded like a most joyous occasion inside the living room.

Only later did I discover the mystery woman was my Mom's sister and her husband, who had come to visit because Mom was pregnant with my soon-to-arrive sister, Peggy.

Daniel 4:5 (NASB) ... "I saw a dream and it made me fearful; and these fantasies as I lay on my bed and the visions in my mind kept alarming me."

Only months later, I watched in confusion and with tears dripping down my cheeks as two men dressed in white coats strapped my mom's hands together. Echoes bolted through my little body with every scream that screeched from Mom's mouth in protest as she was involuntarily being dragged away. Mom was committed to the psychiatric ward of Jacobi Hospital because of her drinking problem.

Dad became an on-and-off again single parent with eight children because Mom would now spend weeks and frequently months in the psychiatric ward.

One day, I was sitting in the last bedroom at the end of the long hallway in our five-bedroom apartment, which was the largest apartment in the building. Besides being the largest apartment, we also had two bathrooms; the other apartments had only one. In years to come, my friends envied our two bathroom luxury. Straining my eardrums from my bedroom down the hall, I could hear Dad's words as he greeted a stranger at the front door. The stranger was a woman who Dad immediately invited into our apartment, and they continued to chat as they both headed in the direction of my room.

Instinctively, I knew that Dad was scheming something. I started to tremble in fear of the unknown and the inevitable that I knew was coming. As Dad came into my bedroom, I was in full-blown, out-of-control rage as I jumped up and down on the bed, screaming and hollering. After a few strong whacks to my behind, my tantrum immediately stopped.

Dad introduced me to the lady with him. "Johnny, this is Anna." Anna was a social worker from the city who would help care for us while Dad was at work.

I began where I left off with my tantrum, screaming and yelling at the top of my lungs. But it was vital for Dad to get to his job being the sole provider for eight children, so he walked right out the door. I just crouched up on my bed sobbing in tears.

Isaiah 43:19 (NIV) ... "See, I am doing a new thing! Now it springs up; do you not perceive it? I am making a way in the wilderness and streams in the wasteland."

My heart was still frozen toward Anna, but within a few days and much talk of taking me on an "adventurer trip," Anna won me over. That day came, and we waited in line at the bus stop. As the bus pulled in, it stopped at a place where the exhaust was being pumped straight into my face. As I choked and coughed nonstop, Anna frantically placed her handkerchief over my nose and mouth, trying to keep the fumes from causing me any more harm. When we were at last safely on the city bus, we headed for Parkchester (another housing project located just past the Castle Hill train station), to which the #6 train traveled in and out of Manhattan.

During the 20-minute journey, I observed the city bus had large, soft, comfortable cushioned seats where I squatted on my knees for the entire ride, watching in wonder as people entered the bus and deposited coins into a boxy looking gadget that sucked the money down into the bus floor. Anna lifted me into the air so I could pull the cord, prompting the bus to stop as we reached our destination.

Together we walked hand-in-hand toward a small circular park that was full of life with a large water fountain smack in the middle of it. We sat on a bench, and I watched in fascination as the large water fountain shot high into the air and came crashing back to the ground. This fountain was gigantic compared to the one in our neighborhood. The sun was warm on my face, and I watched the birds gliding from tree to tree, and the squirrels chasing each other across the grass and up the tree trunks. Life was thrilling, and the only thing on my mind was that moment in time! I could only think about what was in front of me. What I was to do next or what had developed a few minutes before did not exist in my mind.

Anna, looking down at me with a huge smile on her face, pulled four slices of white bread out of a brown paper bag she had in a pocketbook and said, "Johnny, would you like to feed the pigeons? " She tossed the bread on my lap, and within seconds, hundreds of dirty New York pigeons swarmed around us. I could no longer see the large fountain, Anna, the squirrels, or the birds—only pigeons, and they were all over my body.

Quickly, Anna grabbed the slices from me and threw the bread toward the fountain. The pigeons scurried in that direction and away from us. Laughing almost hysterically, Anna reached into her pocketbook and pulled out some tissues to wipe slimy pigeon poop from my head, arms, and legs.

During the ride home, I could feel the vibration of the road underneath the large, soft cushions, and all I could think about at the moment was the coins being sucked down through the boxy gadget into the bus floor and the taste of a salty flavor in my mouth from the slimy pigeon poop.

Esther 9:28 (KJV) ... "And that these days should be remembered and kept throughout every generation, every family, every province, and every city;

and that these days of Purim should not fail from among the Jews, nor the memorial of them perish from their seed."

In those early days, "the projects," as we called them, were under massive construction as I have already mentioned, so there was always plenty of activity in the streets. Of course, two of my very best buddies were named "Mr. Mud and Mr. Dirt," and we were well acquainted.

From my bedroom window, I would look out with frenzy excitement as the gigantic cement trucks poured cement from a large spinning drum down a chute into wheelbarrows for the new sidewalk, stretching from Seward Avenue to our building's side door. Before the new sidewalk was finished, we would have to walk through ankle-deep, slimy mud to get into our building.

Song of Solomon 5:5 (NIV) ... "I arose to open for my beloved, and my hands dripped with myrrh, my fingers with flowing myrrh, on the handles of the bolt."

As the sidewalk was being poured from Seward Avenue to our side building's entrance, I had a fantastic view. Perched on the square ledge of my wide-open bedroom window, I watched rugged men in knee-high boots tracking through the cement, using long poles as if they were egg beaters, mixing and spreading the cement.

I had one thought: "How long will it be before those workers leave so I can jump from this window ledge, track through the mud, and get to that wet cement?" Then as quickly as possible, I would dig both of my palms face down into the cement, leaving my imprint.

However, on this particular day, I was too quick, and not realizing the cement had been poured only moments before, I slid both of my hands into the deep cement, and the momentum carried my body forward as both knees, then my chest, elbows and stomach landed flat into the pool of wet cement. When I stood up, my whole body was covered in cement; I could feel wet cement dripping from my hair onto my face.

I turned, and to my horror, watching from the kitchen window was Mom. She screamed, "Don't move! Stay right where you are!" Mom jumped from the kitchen window, and within minutes, she was stripping me down to my underwear. She then had me embarrassingly walk into the building, wearing only my underwear.

For the next few years, as the St. John Vianney School and private houses in the neighborhood were being built, the construction sites in the area became an electrifying wonderland filled with dirty fun and excitement for us.

Ecclesiastes 11:9 (NLT) ... "Young people, it's wonderful to be young! Enjoy every minute of it. Do everything you want to do; take it all in. But remember that you must give an account to God for everything."

A couple of 300-ton dump trucks, along with a few 50-ton bulldozers, were parked right across the street from our building. The magnetic attraction those big rigs had on my older brothers, our friends, and me was overwhelming.

We ran across the street, all knowing the last one to the heavy machinery was a "rotten egg"! We pushed, pulled, kicked, punched, and tried to hold each other back in order to get up on the driver's seat first. After slipping past a few of the older guys, I made it first to the top of a bulldozer and onto the driver's seat.

Excited and proud of myself, I boasted of my accomplishment to the boys below, screaming loudly, "I'm king of the hill!" In all of the commotion and drama, my attention was diverted, and I slipped off the driver's seat. My face slammed full force onto the pool-ball-sized stick shift. My right eye took the brunt of the fall, and, to make matters worse, the gobs of grease on the handle of the stick shift filled my watery eye.

I ran home screaming and crying in pain, with an apprehensive trail of onlookers, following right behind me into our apartment. The injury certainly put an exclamation point on my day, but I survived!

Psalm 120:4 (NIV) … "He will punish you with a warrior's sharp arrows, with burning coals of the broom bush."

Unfortunately, my short life still wasn't finished with damaging my right eye. One day, Tommy and Billy, two of my brothers and I were climbing the large sycamore tree just outside our kitchen window to load up on our "ammunition"—"itchy balls"—the seed pods from the sycamore tree. Itchy balls are about an inch-and-a-half across with sharp spines sticking out like a porcupine.

We would wait for unsuspecting targets to enter the building and then launch our attack. Itchy balls were easy to throw and would burst on impact, sticking to its victims and causing them to scratch and itch. We were abruptly interrupted when Dad's car pulled into a parking space on Seward Avenue. Dad yelled our names, and in unison, we bolted toward the car.

From the trunk of his car, he pulled out wooden bow and arrows and handed a set to each of us. The arrows had rubber tips to prevent injury, but we removed them in order to inflict more pain and damage to the small rodents and birds that we imagined ourselves hunting down.

Like a warrior, my brother, Tommy, pulled back his bow as far as possible and released his arrow. I nonchalantly turned toward him just in time to see the arrow headed straight for my face. I tried to jump out of the way with no success. Suddenly, SPLAT! My right eye once again took the brunt, only this time from an arrow. The stars I saw at that moment were too numerous to count, and once again, I ran home screaming and crying in agony, with an apprehensive trail of onlookers following right behind me into our apartment.

None of these traumatic injuries stayed with me for very long. Like most kids, I forgot about the pain as soon as I had something else to occupy my curious mind. Only later would I discover the devastating long-term consequences of these injuries.

Colossians 3:21 (NIV) … "Fathers, do not embitter your children, or they will become discouraged."

When I was old enough for kindergarten, my parents prepared me for my first day of school. To fancy me up and make a handsome boy out of me, they spread and combed gobs of Vaseline throughout my hair. My head felt as if I was wearing a bronze metal helmet weighing ten pounds, but they accomplished their task. My hair stayed in place and wouldn't move.

But once I was at school, they didn't bargain for my less-than-enthusiastic response! As my parents took me into the kindergarten class, my heart was pumping with a mixture of fear and anticipation. Right then and there, I decided that school was not for me. I began screaming, kicking, and yelling, not wanting to be left alone with a bunch of strangers. Then in one motion, I jerked my desk into the teacher's, causing a fishbowl to come flying off her desk and crash onto the floor. As the goldfish were flipping and flopping on the floor, I momentarily stopped and watched as they struggled and gasped for air.

Snapping out from my daydream about the goldfish, I continued my tantrum, until at last the teacher had no choice but to send me home with my parents.

Genesis 1:27 (NIV) … "So God created man in his own image, in the image of God he created him; male and female he created them."

When I did finally make it back to school for the first grade, things hadn't changed much considering I still received the Vaseline hair treatment. First grade imaging is dull and blah for me, but I will struggle through.

One highlight was the girl named Kim, a petite quiet black girl who sat directly in front of me. I did take notice that Kim was the only black kid in my class, and I often imagined what it might be like to be a different color. I thought of it as both good and bad. On the one hand, I thought she was somehow "special." On the other, she was considered "different." The color difference only lasted for the moment and faded fast as she just became "Kim" to me.

The classroom environment was weird to me because I just couldn't grasp the whole idea of why I was there. Eventually, my seat was changed from behind Kim because I had a habit of kicking the back of her chair. Sitting in one place for long periods of time agitated me.

Sarah was the girl I would snuggle next to in the school theater when we would watch documentaries on the big screen Friday mornings during the weekly assembly. After we became good friends, Sarah let me in on one of her very private secrets: she was terrified of fire. I consoled her and even held her hand, assuring her no fire would come to the theater while we watched the documentaries.

I didn't think much of it at the time, but as I was telling my brother Billy about her little secret, he had a much different view other than holding her hand and consoling her. Sarah lived in the 2140 building across from our building, facing the three mountains. I didn't know what *extortion* was then, but I was about to find out. I was told to follow him because "We are about to make some money."

I didn't ask questions but just followed Billy over to 2140 as we stood in the grass below Sarah's fourth-floor apartment window.

Billy yelled at the top of his lungs for Sarah to come to the window, and after about five minutes of loud screaming, she raised the window and stuck out her head. Billy said, "Bring any money you can find in your house and throw it out the window to me."

Her answer was a nervous "NO."

Billy shouted back, "Sarah, don't test me!" But she still insisted, "NO." Billy then whispered to me, on his cue, to run toward the other side of the building where Sarah would not be able to see me. He then said in a serious voice, "Sarah, unless you throw money out of the window, we will burn down your house." Sarah was now in a panic but refused to throw money out of the window. Billy whispered for me to run to the other side of the building out of sight. Billy then looked in my direction and shouted, "Light it up!"

Crying hysterically, Sarah then shouted, "Okay! Okay!" She disappeared into her window and minutes later she began throwing change down to us.

This extortion became a monthly ritual until she moved out of the projects shortly afterward, and our "cash cow" quickly disappeared.

Ephesians 4:29 (NLT) … "Don't use foul or abusive language. Let everything you say be good and helpful, so that your words will be an encouragement to those who hear them…."

My first memory of reading centered on a book with characters named "Dick" and "Jane." The first word I remember reading out loud was the word "said." To my fascination, it rolled off my tongue, exploding into the air. I repeated "said" all day long—just shooting it from my lips like a bullet from a gun.

I also learned another word from the neighborhood kids in front of our building. This particular word was such a vile, filthy curse word, it was not even spoken verbally, only spelled out. Unfortunately for me, I had absolutely no understanding that the word was inappropriate to use in any way. I knew just enough about spelling to go home and write out the alphabet letters to spell the word I had heard on a piece of paper. Then I tried several times to pronounce the word I had heard—while sitting right in front of my dad. Yup, he was angry, and I was disciplined. The only word rolling off my tongue after that day was "said."

Another day, I drifted outside of the house, sat on the benches between our two buildings, and began listening to the song "Downtown" by Petula Clark, which was blasting from a transistor radio held by one of the older guys. I recognized that the guys on the bench were from 2140. I watched as they joked and whispered while looking toward a short, chubby-looking kid heading in our direction. "Hey, Mitchell! Get over here!" one of the guys shouted.

Mitchell sprinted over with a big smile on his face. "What's up, guys?"

One of them asked, "You can sing, right?"

Mitchell answered "Yes."

They proceeded to ask him to sing the song "Downtown." As Mitchell started to sing, I couldn't believe it. He sounded exactly like the lady who was singing the song on the radio. He was great! When he finished singing the song, they asked him to sing it again...and again...and again for about fifteen minutes.

I loved it because I enjoyed the song. Mitchell finally spoke up and said, "My voice is beginning to hurt. I want to go home."

The guys wouldn't let him. They made him stand there singing the song for about thirty minutes as tears were rolling down his cheeks. As he started to sing the song another time, even as a first grader, I knew Mitchell was in pain, but he was trapped in the claws of these evil guys. I walked back to my building only thinking that I was very lucky that I did not know how to sing.

Genesis 1:12 (KJV) … "And the earth brought forth grass, the herb that yields seed according to its kind, and the tree that yields fruit, whose seed is in itself according to its kind. And God saw that it was good."

If you have been to the Bronx in the last twenty years, you may be a little surprised when I tell you that, in the early 1960s, there was still plenty of open space. Acres lush with trees, bushes, and shrubs provided homes for small critters such as snakes, mice, rabbits, turtles and squirrels. Three gigantic rock mountains were only a short distance from our building behind 2140. Not being very creative, we called these rock outcroppings "the first mountain," "the second mountain," and "the third mountain." Each was separated by the trees, water, and other vegetation along with plenty of swamp land.

I had learned to imitate what the older guys did to Mitchell, so one day while at the mountains, I got together with a younger and weaker kid than myself. For thirty minutes or so, I made him follow me through thorn bushes, weeds, and then up and down the second mountain while having him sing the song "Downtown" to me. Finally, I couldn't take his voice any longer. Frustrated that he couldn't sing as well as Mitchell, I just turned to him and shouted, "Shut up!" Then I sent him home.

Later that year, I saw that same boy, only this time, he was very brittle and weak and seated in a wheelchair. He passed away soon afterward from a disease called leukemia, and my thoughts always went back to his singing version of "Downtown." Only these times in my mind, his voice sounded sweet and gentle. I would always appreciate the short time we spent together.

Psalm 118:12 (NIV) ... *"They swarmed around me like bees, but they were consumed as quickly as burning thorns; in the name of the* LORD *I cut them down."*

My older brother, Tommy, and his friends would take me on "adventures," or maybe better said, "hiking on the three mountains." They would hunt snakes, turtles, and other rodents, but I wasn't interested in any of those critters. I liked the little wings, long stingers, and buzzing sounds of bees! Hives of bumblebees and yellow jacket spread throughout the beautiful flowers, which grew plentifully in the green grass around the mountains. I would sneak up on an unsuspecting bee and clap my hands together, killing the bee instantly.

Yes, I admit it. I was a "bee clapper"—until the day when I clapped my hands together around the wrong bee. This little tough guy's stinger went straight into my palm. As I jumped back in pain, I tripped and fell directly onto a bee hive. I watched in fear as my hand swelled, and hundreds of bees began circling my brothers and me. This time everyone ran home, screaming and crying in pain as we were being chased and stung by the bees. The apprehensive trail of onlookers following me were now participants in my pain. That was my last time clapping at a bee!

GUMBY

▲ ▲ ▲

PROVERBS 18:24 (ESV) ... "A man of many companions may come to ruin, but there is a friend who sticks closer than a brother."

Tommy G. was one of our first friends in the housing projects. Tommy lived on the eleventh floor, which was a great reason alone to be his friend. Looking out of his eleventh-floor bedroom window was a breathtaking view of Castle Hill Avenue. You could see the gigantic smoke stacks at the sanitation department and the Whitestone Bridge stretching across the river to the borough of Queens. The LaGuardia Airport flight path was right above his window, and it felt as if you could just grab an airplane flying overhead. And to watch something, such as a water balloon or an egg, drop from the window and fall eleven stories to the ground was really fascinating—especially if it happened to land on a person's head!

Tommy eventually earned the nickname of "Gumby" because he moved as if he was made of rubber like the cartoon character and because Gumby sounded a bit like his last name. The nicknames that were made up came from the humor of one of the C. brothers, who all had a strange sense of humor. They nicknamed my older brother Billy and me "Muz-Buz," which later in life was shortened to just "Muz." My brother, Tommy, was nicknamed "Worm," and our friend Jerry had the moniker "Wiggles."

Luke 7:36 (NASB) ... "Now one of the Pharisees was requesting Him to dine with him, and he entered the Pharisee's house and reclined at the table."

Gumby's dad, Mr. G., made awesome and delicious chocolate egg creams—a mixture of milk, syrup, and seltzer water. Mr. G. would sit down with us, like he was one of the boys, and just enjoy our company. We sipped homemade egg creams and munched on cookies in his kitchen as we waved frantically at the passengers on board the passing airplanes. As our imaginations ran away with us, we believed one day we would have the honor to fly. Our little minds could not wrap around it when Gumby's Dad said, "They serve food and have a bathroom on each flight."

My brother Billy laughed and wondered out loud, "Does the toilet flush open below, spilling its waste onto people in the streets?"

After Mr. G. fed us, it was usually time to burn off some of the high energy those cookies gave us. Gumby, Billy, and I would race each other out the door, bolting down the stairs from the eleventh floor to the first floor. We laughed, joked and screamed all the way down while trying to hold each other back from reaching the ground floor. Sometimes if we had a cardboard box, we would sit on it and slide down the stairs. Whoever made it to the ground floor first was declared the winner and had extreme bragging rights for the moment. Then we would explode from the building lobby, race down toward the construction sites, and the same prize, "extreme bragging rights," awaited the winner.

Mr. G. would soon do a confusing thing in my young innocent eyes. He walked out, deserting his wife and children. Only later in life did I realize the devastating effect it had on our friend, Tommy, and his family.

Judges 20:16 (NASB) … "Out of all these people 700 choice men were left-handed; each one could sling a rock at a hair and not miss."

The new homes under construction by the mountains had a fascinating appeal for us kids. We would patiently wait until all of the construction workers left for the day, and then we would begin our mischief. Our mission was who could find the biggest rock and break the biggest window. The excitement was overbearing. Gumby was the only person I knew of who was left-handed; in my eyes, it was a special gift he had. I was usually the smallest kid, so I had to get really close to the houses if my selected rock was to reach the targeted window.

Lining up and taking aim, Gumby, standing behind me, picked up the biggest and heaviest rock he could find. He would be the first to throw his rock at one of the top floor windows. From behind me, I could hear him mumbling something about his humongous strength, bragging on and on about his super powers. But with all that immense, super strength, he didn't bargain for his rock to lose speed and lift and land right into the back of my head. I saw stars and became light-headed as I fell to the ground with blood gushing from the back of my head.

This time I was carried home in a fog with an apprehensive trail of onlookers following me right into our apartment. The next thing I remember was the sound of the ambulance siren outside my building, and having my head stitched right there on the couch in our living room. As of this writing, the scar still remains on the back of my head.

Luke 23:34 (ESV) … "And Jesus said, 'Father, forgive them, for they know not what they do.' And they cast lots to divide his garments."

I was still in the first grade when my brothers decided I should skip school with them and a few other boys. We were halfway to school when the decision was made, so we turned and headed in the opposite direction, camping out near the first mountain. So, there I was—a future juvenile delinquent playing hooky from the first grade. Our elementary school was about three blocks away from the first moun-tain, and at lunch time, we could hear our principal's voice drifting through the air currents as he made the daily announcements over the school loudspeaker.

Throughout the day, we continued to run into small packs of other kids from different parts of the projects who were also play-ing hooky. My brother, Tommy, looking to have a little fun with me, said the principal was speaking directly to me, warning me he was on his way to the mountain with the police to put me in jail for playing hooky.

Boy, did his announcement really ruin my day! I spent the rest of the afternoon, looking over my shoulder and getting neck cramps while waiting for the principal to jump out from behind a tree, grab me by my collar, and haul me off to jail! Worse than that was fear-fully looking at my dad that evening during dinner, knowing I had played hooky and thinking he would surely find out.

Leviticus 19:18 (KJV) … "Thou shalt not avenge, nor bear any grudge against the children of thy people, but thou shalt love thy neighbour as thy-self: I am the LORD."

Our friends, the C. family, lived on the twelfth floor of our building, and they had a large family like ours—four girls and four boys. The

C. boys were the ones with the real strange sense of humor that, to this day, I am sure rubbed off on my family, our other friends, and even me.

I can remember my first encounter with Tommy and Mary C. I was with my brother, Billy, in the street, and we saw Tommy and Mary standing next to their father's car. Billy walked right over and started harassing Tommy, pushing and teasing him. Suddenly his sister, Mary, came running from the other side of the car; she shoved Billy, jolting him backward into the trunk. Then she exploded lunging towards me with what felt like sharp claws scratching at my face and shoulders.

We took off running as Mary screamed at us, "Run, cowards, run!" That Mary was one fierce, tough cookie! After we became friends with the family, I found out that Tommy and Mary were actually twins, and that really didn't make sense to me because I didn't understand that twins could be different genders. Mr. C. would always park his car on Seward Avenue with the car doors unlocked.

One time, without Mr. C.'s knowledge, we crawled around inside of his car. On that day, we put the gear shift into neutral and then released the emergency brake. He had parked on a hill, and we watched in horror as it rolled and slammed into the back of another car, busting its headlights.

I securely watched from the comfort of my window ledge as Tommy and Mary were scolded and took blame for our mishap. That was the last time we ever played inside Mr. C's car!

Isaiah 14:12 (NIV) ... *"How you have fallen from heaven, morning star, son of the dawn! You have been cast down to the earth, you who once laid low the nations!"*

One day when we were sitting on the benches outside the building with the C. family, I ventured off to the park for some mischief with Patricia

C. who was a few years younger than me. As we entered the park, our choice of recreation turned out to be the seesaws. I sat on one end of the seesaw, and Patricia, with a excited smile on her face, sat on the other end.

After a few minutes of this up-and-down activity, I thought I would tease and scare her. So when it was my turn to touch the ground again, I held her up in the air, laughing as I kept my weight anchored to the ground. Listening to her laughter turn into cries because I would not bring her down, I continued to laugh as she begged me to lower her end of the seesaw. "Are you really sure you want to come down?" I asked.

"Yes! Please let me down!" she cried as her eyes were swelling with tears pouring down from her cheeks.

So without any understanding of the severe consequences that were about to happen, I just said, "Okay," and with one motion stood up, which quickly released her weight to the inevitable pull of gravity. She came screaming down to the ground, smashing her face into the metal handle of the seesaw. Her chin split wide open, and blood splattered everywhere.

Isaiah 41:10 (AKJV) … "Fear thou not; for I am with thee: be not dismayed; for I am thy God: I will strengthen thee; yea, I will help thee; yea, I will uphold thee with the right hand of my righteousness."

Panicking, I immediately took off my shirt, grabbed Patricia, and held the shirt against her chin to stop the bleeding. I looked at the large gash in her chin and almost passed out myself. Together, we ran toward the benches where our families sat talking.

What felt like minutes later, I was holding the lobby door open as the ambulance drivers rushed into the elevator and up to the twelfth floor where Patricia was waiting to get her stitches. Before long, as

I waited in the hallway outside the C,'s family apartment, I realized the sense of humor the C. brothers normally had was gone. Now only anger filled their eyes, and those eyes pointed straight in my direction. They chased me from the twelfth floor all the way down to the first floor, running all the way down the stairs and screaming about how they were going to kick my backside for what I had done to Patricia.

Luckily for me, I made it into my apartment only steps away from being devoured. For the rest of my life, Patricia never let me forget that day. Whenever I would see her, she would always point to the lifetime scar left on her chin from that day, and being such a forgiving person, she would just smile.

Exodus 32:19 (NLT) ... "When they came near the camp, Moses saw the calf and the dancing, and he burned with anger. He threw the stone tablets to the ground, smashing them at the foot of the mountain."

After my sister, Peggy, was born, I noticed my mother started drinking lots of alcohol. She had delivered and tended to eight wild children, and maybe the stress of rearing such a large family was too much. Mom would sit at the kitchen table with a glass of beer in one hand and a cigarette in the other, raising her arm high in the air while singing old sailor bar songs, encouraging us to sing along. When she was upset at Dad, those old sailor bar songs would turn into nasty songs about his sleeping with "sleazy fat woman with big breasts."

Mom and Dad would get into some loud screaming matches about her drinking problem. During the day, when Dad was at work, Mom would leave and walk across Castle Hill Avenue to the delicatessen and buy beer. Unbeknownst to Dad, she would run up the grocery tab and then hide her extra unfinished beer somewhere in the house before Dad came home.

When Dad got home from work, he routinely asked my brother Jimmy and me, "Where did she hide the beer?" Mom knew the drill, so she would try to bribe us with cookies she had bought at the store, hoping we wouldn't tell Dad when he got home. But if Dad couldn't find the beer and he got angry enough, Jimmy and I would chirp like baby birds. At the same time we would regurgitate the cookies we had finished not long before, while showing Dad exactly where the beer was hidden. Dad would then smash the bottles of beer in the sink while shouting ugly profanities at Mom.

Proverbs 24:16 (KJV) … "For a just man falleth seven times, and riseth up again: but the wicked shall fall into mischief."

There were also some memorable good times. Mom loved to take us on picnics, and we loved to go. Indeed, her idea of a picnic was a bit unusual. Mom would open the kitchen window, and Jimmy and I would climb out onto the grass. She would hand us a blanket, and we would spread it out. Next Mom would pass the Kool-Aid and peanut butter and jelly sandwiches, and then she would close the window. After a few beers, Mom sometimes would get silly and climb out of the window, holding a beer in one hand and a cigarette in the other. She would sit on the grass and join us.

Every now and then, Ernie, who lived on the third floor above us, would pour cold water down on us, and our picnic would get "rained" out. Ernie really enjoyed sticking his head out of their third-floor apartment window. One day, when I was sitting in my bedroom looking out my window, I heard a loud "thump!" in the grass. What I saw next was shocking. Ernie had fallen three stories from his window. After a few moments of me thinking Ernie was dead, he stood up and walked straight over to my window with a big smile on his face, indicating he was okay. I couldn't wait to see his mom's face when she found out he had fallen out his window.

I flew out of my window and joined him for a race up to the third floor. After knocking on his door, and his mom had answered, she immediately screamed, realizing what had happened. After she had examined him and saw that he was fine, her hand blazed like lightning through the air, slapping him on the backside with a harsh warning about hanging out of his bedroom window.

I remember thinking, "Ernie just fell out of a third-floor window. Does his mom really think a slap on the butt would hurt him? HE'S SUPERMAN!"

I was broadcasting the news all day to anyone who would listen. "ERNIE FELL OUT OF HIS THIRD-FLOOR WINDOW!"

Ironically, today Ernie jumps from airplanes, teaching students how to parachute.

James 5:6 (ESV) ... "You have condemned and murdered the righteous person. He does not resist you."

President John F. Kennedy was assassinated while I was in the first grade, and the memory of his death will last a lifetime. I clearly recall the day he was assassinated. Another teacher quietly whispered to our teacher to step into the hallway. She couldn't have been gone for more than a minute or two when we began to hear loud weeping and wailing right outside the classroom door.

When our teacher returned to the classroom, she was shaking and in tears. She was desperately trying to gather her emotions and catch her breath to talk to her class of young students. At last, when we could bear the suspense no longer, she quietly said, "The President has been shot."

In stunned silence, our class filed into the hallway to be sent home. We instinctively knew this single event had significant meaning, yet we were too young to understand exactly how. For me, getting the weekend started off earlier than usual was the highlight of my day.

That week another image was burned into my memory as I listened to my brothers and our father discuss in detail of how the bullet that hit the President blew off half of his head. I watched the news over and over, showing the motorcade up to the point of the incident and then watching his wife jump in hysterical panic from the back of the convertible into the street. That night, after listening to my brothers and Dad's discussion, I slept a little closer to my brother, Billy, with my eyes wide open, trying to get those scary images out of my head.

Only as an adult, did I find out that one of my heroes for the Christian faith, C.S. Lewis, also died on that day. C. S. wrote a book entitled *The Screwtape Letters*, which forever changed my perspective of Satan. But that day of the JFK assassination overshadowed all of the other news.

1 Corinthians 14:33 (NASB) ... "for God is not a God of confusion but of peace, as in all the churches of the saints."

The world seemed as if it was turned upside down over the next few days as adults tried, in vain, to find an explanation for the events. The death of President John F. Kennedy was surely the most momentous time of my short life. Up to that point, I remember the President was involved with the Russians about missiles in Cuba, and this was the reason we were having so many air-raid drills in school. This dialogue would become known as the "Cuban Missile Crisis."

Sirens would blare throughout the school and each class had to quietly file into the stairwell. We would stand there quietly for practice; it was a drill to hopefully keep us safe in case the Russians fired nuclear bombs at us. The drills made no sense to me because I had no idea what a nuclear missile was, let alone what Russians were. Our nation was in mourning up until the next amazing event that would appear.

Matthew 18:3(NIV) … "And he said: 'Truly I tell you, unless you change and become like little children, you will never enter the kingdom of heaven.' "

Sunday nights at our house were always special as we would, with great anticipation, watch "The Ed Sullivan Show." It was a family tradition. My father would gather us around our black-and-white television set, and we would anxiously wait for whatever Ed had in store that week. He always had some weird act on like singing monkeys or comedians or flying acrobats.

But this one particular Sunday night is indelibly imprinted in my memory. That night, as we settled in for our weekly viewing, four mop-top guys began singing to a crowded theater full of screaming, out-of-control, teenage girls. I watched in amazement as our living room came alive, and the Beatles unexpectedly became the national remedy for our dark period of mourning. It wasn't simply four guys singing in harmony; the sound was so different from anything we had ever before heard. The death of John Kennedy was no longer the top news and quickly faded from my mind.

Psalm 119:1 (NCV) … "Happy are those who live pure lives, who follow the LORD's teachings."

The next day we were running down the hallway singing the Beatles' song, "I Want to Hold Your Hand." Billy and I jumped into the elevator and ran it straight up to the eleventh floor, where we banged loudly on Gumby's door calling for him to come out. He opened the door with an expression of pure excitement on his face. "Did you guys see that last night?" He had caught the "Beatlemania" fever too!

The three of us took off down the stairs, laughing and giggling like little girls, while we sang another Beatles' song, "She loves you, yeah, yeah, yeah…" Between floors, each staircase had fourteen steps until the next floor then, a sharp turn and another fourteen steps. This pattern continued all the way to the first floor.

As we reached the eighth floor, my sneaker came untied, and as we rounded the turn going from the eighth floor to the seventh floor, Gumby stepped on my loose shoelace, sending me tripping head first at the top of the stairs. Gumby fell on top of me, and Billy followed in turn falling on top of Gumby. All of us fell down the stairs together, banging our heads, legs and arms until we reached the landing on the seventh floor. We came to a stop bunched up together in the corner next to the exit door. We laid there moaning and groaning, no longer singing delightful Beatle songs. Screeching in pain, we decided, at that moment, as we crawled into the seventh floor hallway, the elevator was the better choice to the lobby.

Matthew 6:11 (NIV) … "Give us today our daily bread."

Breakfast on Sunday mornings always consisted of buttered rolls and tea. The taste of a buttered roll dipped into a hot cup of tea was as delicious to us as any gourmet meal prepared for a king. Admittedly, the oily, wet bread crumbs floating on top of the tea after dipping the buttered roll looked a little disgusting.

Each Sunday one of the clan would be sent out early to the delicatessen on Castle Hill Avenue. The deli was directly across the street from the 20-story building 635, in a strip mall that we simply called "the stores." The strip mall also had a liquor store, a luncheonette, a drug store, a department store, a food store, and a stairway leading down behind the stores to a row of shops in the back, including a hair salon, a Laundromat, and a boxing gym. The stairway leading to the back of the stores would be used by the teenagers at times to sing doo-wop songs in harmony, entertaining onlookers passing through. Doo-wop is a style of music from the late 50s and early 60s, and if sung with the right harmony would send chills up and down your spine.

Daniel 3:24 (NIV) ... "Then King Nebuchadnezzar leaped to his feet in amazement and asked his advisers, 'Weren't there three men that we tied up and threw into the fire?' They replied, 'Certainly, Your Majesty.' "

I distinctly remember visions in my mind that the three men working behind the counter in the delicatessen looked like funny cartoon characters. One was tall and skinny, the other was short and fat, and the third was about ninety-nine years old, or so he seemed to me. They were very strict, like military guards, and if you stepped out of the line that stretched out the doorway into the street, you were sent to the back of the line. That always seemed to happen to me! When your turn came to give your order, you had to be quick and precise, or they would somehow find a way to embarrass you. To total your bill, they would use the side of the brown paper bag into which they placed your groceries. With a pencil stub, they would write down each item you bought, scratching the name and the price in order. Then the items were tallied, and a total was written at the bottom.

This process always amazed me because sometimes they would have to add fifteen to twenty items, and they always made it look so easy. Every now and then when I saw they were in deep concentration counting, I would start counting out loud to confuse them. That's generally when I would be sent to the back of the line.

1 Corinthians 14:40 (ESV) … "But all things should be done decently and in order."

On Sunday mornings, Dorothy or Tommy usually had to make the trip to pick up our order. And the order was always the same: two dozen Kaiser rolls, four quarts of milk, and the Sunday newspaper. Dad had to have the newspaper every day, or he was lost. Every night except Sunday, one of us would have to go out at 9:00 p.m. to get the *Daily News Night Owl*.

When I was a little older and inherited the job of being the runner for the rolls on Sunday mornings, I figured it would be much quicker if I took my bicycle. This particular week, I was practicing riding my bike with no hands, and it had become a simple task. Having perfected my talent, I decided to put it to a real test. Leaving the delicatessen, I would now attempt riding my bike with no hands while holding the rolls, a newspaper, and four quarts of milk.

Proverbs 16:18 (MSG) … "First pride, then the crash— the bigger the ego, the harder the fall."

I was doing great and was quite proud of myself when halfway home, the bike began to wobble; the front wheel suddenly turned completely around. It was as if someone had immediately slammed on the brakes. The bike, the rolls, the newspaper, four quarts of milk, and of course, me, were now airborne. At that moment, I saw everything in slow motion. The shopping bag slipped below my waist as the items inside took off in different directions. I had now become my childhood hero, "Superman,"—flying through the air, frantically waving my arms, with the bicycle directly behind, knowing it was about to land right on top of me after the crash. Hitting the hard, cold pavement, my body slid a few feet, peeling the hide from my elbows and knees. I laid on the sidewalk in puddles of milk, with my bicycle on top of me, watching the rolls rolling everywhere, and the newspaper being blown away by the heavy wind.

I now had two major concerns at the moment: 1) Did anyone see this embarrassing debacle, and 2) How am I going to explain this disaster to Dad?

Ephesians 5:4 (NIV) ... "Nor should there be obscenity, foolish talk or coarse joking, which are out of place, but rather thanksgiving."

When the Sunday order arrived, we would boil water in a large pot to make tea. We would add four tea bags to make ten cups of tea, and everyone would wait with anticipation for the feast to begin. We joked and teased one another over our tea and buttered rolls all around the table, but the teasing was mostly directed toward Billy.

Tommy and Dorothy would claim that Billy had a girlfriend named Alisah, who lived in the next building. Billy would always end up having a tantrum with tears, physical fighting, screaming profanities, running up and down the hallway, dashing in and out of the bedrooms. The last stop would be a bathroom door slamming shut. Lots of loud noises screeched throughout the apartment when things got heated. This circus atmosphere lasted only to a certain point.

When Dad could no longer take the fighting, off would come his belt. Like magic, the house would simmer down, and all that could be heard was the dunking of rolls into our tea, along with the slobbering sucking sounds of digested bread and hot caffeinated water going into our bellies.

Matthew 7:7 (NIV) ... "Ask and it will be given to you; seek and you will find; knock and the door will be opened to you."

Gumby had a secret knock for our door—"Tap, tap, tap, tap, tap, a pause, then tap-tap." No matter who answered his taps, the question was always the same: "Are Johnny and Billy here?" Even if I answered the door or if Billy peered out in answer to his taps, Gumby would still say "Are Johnny and Billy here?"

Gumby was a real joker. Calling on a friend had a special aura about it as one knock usually turned into a mob of kids. The escalating assembly normally worked like this: Gumby would call on Billy and me. The three of us would call on Brian. The four of us would call on the C.'s, and at least two of the brothers would come out. Then the six of us would call on Jerry. On and on and on it went. Some days we would wind up with twelve to fifteen guys together within a fifteen-minute period.

But I also remember the times of knocking on door after door with either no answer or only to find that friend unable to come out to burn off some energy. Such times invited a touch of loneliness, which only lasted until I walked back into our apartment where either brothers and/or sisters were home to help burn off that excess energy.

Numbers 3:51 (NIV) ... "Moses gave the redemption money to Aaron and his sons, as he was commanded by the word of the LORD."

Before we left for church on Sunday, we always had to go see Dad to get the money for the church donation basket. The last bedroom down the hall on the left was Dad's room. He would usually be lying down with his shirt hitched up over his belly, watching a western movie on television. "Don't forget to bring home the church bulletin," he would say and then give us each twenty-five cents for the donation basket. Billy and I would stand outside Dad's bedroom door for a few minutes each Sunday, hoping he would fall back asleep. When loud snoring would indicate he was sleeping like a baby, one of us would crawl on his belly beside the bed, reach up to get his wallet sitting on the table beside his bed, and pull out an extra dollar that we would split—if we didn't get caught!

Exodus 20:8 (NIV) … "Remember the Sabbath day by keeping it holy."

Skipping church was normal for us, and as we approached the church, we would argue about who would walk in to get the bulletin to give to Dad as if we had attended church that morning. One Sunday, when it was my turn to get the bulletin, I walked into the church. I stuck out my hand, and a man handed me the church bulletin. I turned toward him with an expression of mock surprise on my face and looked around, "What happened to my father?" I asked."Oh, he must be outside."

With this excuse, I could easily get out of the church and back out onto the street to catch up with Billy and Gumby, who were now about a block away, rushing to get to the candy store. Only this time, the man at the door was on to me and grabbed me by my collar. I twisted to get loose and his arm landed against my mouth so I bit him and took off running. Catching up to Billy and Gumby, I warned them about who the man was so they could be on the lookout for the next time.

We would buy fistfuls of candy, stuff our pockets, and walk around eating our loot, perusing the neighborhood until church was finished. Then we'd go home, full and happy!

Genesis 22:13 (NIV) … "Abraham looked up and there in a thicket he saw a ram caught by its horns. He went over and took the ram and sacrificed it as a burnt offering instead of his son."

One Sunday morning, we were walking back to the church from the candy store still stuffing our faces with candy when Gumby screeched, "Oh, boy! It's your dad!"

Billy stared in disbelief, and I looked up just in time to see and hear Dad screaming at the top of his lungs from the car window, "Why aren't you guys in church?"

As Billy and I scrambled guiltily into the car, Dad motioned for Gumby to join us. Gumby said, "I'd rather walk," but my father gave him a stern look, and without another word, Gumby slid into the seat next to us. Dad's first swing missed me, but the second swing caught me right under my chin. He was driving and slapping us at the same time, and we were ducking, desperately trying to avoid his thunderous blows. When we got to our building, Gumby bolted from the car, ran into the building, and we weren't far behind him.

Matthew 20:16 (NIV) … "So the last will be first, and the first will be last."

Once we were in our apartment, Dad ordered, "Get to your rooms." Still quaking with fear, yet finding humor in the situation, we smothered our laughter behind our hands and waited for our fate to befall us. "You go first," Billy would say, and I would say, "No you go first!" We were talking about who would get hit first. Dad always took his time getting to our room. He knew we were scared to death, and he wanted to build the suspense to a fever pitch. As we would wait in our room for the punishment, Billy would start making funny wisecracks that would lead to serious side-aching laughter. If Dad walked in while we were laughing and we could not control that laughter, his anger level would hit a boiling point.

Jeremiah 13:6 (NIV) … "Many days later the LORD said to me, 'Go now to Perath and get the belt I told you to hide there.' "

As Dad entered the room, the anticipated question was, "Who wants to be first?"

With stupid smiles on our faces, trying hard not to laugh, and hoping to stave off the inevitable, we would each point at the other and say "HIM!"

This time, Dad asked why we didn't go to church, and we both shrugged our shoulders—a gesture he absolutely could not stand. Actually, Dad couldn't stand two things. Besides the shrugging of shoulders routine, he detested looking at me wearing my t-shirt in-side out and backward.

He would yell in my face, "You have your t-shirt on inside out and backward. Go change!"

I would run to the bathroom and change my shirt, hoping I got it right. I had no clue what "inside out and backward" meant. I would just hope after mixing my shirt around a few times that it would come out right. When I would come to stand in front of him for his inspection, he would now yell, "It's still inside out!"

I would dash back to the bathroom to play roulette with my t-shirt until I got it right. It was quite some time before I figured out what "inside out and backward" meant.

Slowly and deliberately, Dad unbuckled his belt. By the look in his eyes, I was fairly sure that I would be first. He whipped me so hard with the buckle that I started to bleed, and I was screaming and yelling for him to stop. When it was over, I was still groaning from the pain, but I looked at Billy with a giggling smirk, knowing I was leaving and that he was next.

Genesis 39:15 (NIV) ... *"When he heard me scream for help, he left his cloak beside me and ran out of the house."*

From down the hall in the living room, we could hear Billy screaming, "Please! I won't do it again!"

Dad said: "Right, you won't! You take my money, play hooky from church, buy candy, and think you're getting away with it?"

As always, we were convicted on all counts—without the benefit of a jury or a trial, and without fail—our sentence was the belt! When Dad had finished, and the correction was all over, I would run back into the room to see how Billy was doing. We would look at each other, and instantaneously both of us would burst into laughter. We examined each other's wounds, trying to determine who got the worst punishment. It became a manly contest with us; whoever got the worst beating between us would be considered the stronger and braver one for the moment.

OLD LADY NANA

▲ ▲ ▲

2 TIMOTHY 1:5 (NIV) … "I have been reminded of your sincere faith, which first lived in your grandmother Lois and in your mother Eunice and, I am persuaded, now lives in you also."

My grandmother, whom we called "Nana," lived about six miles from us, and we would visit her on Sundays. Nana lived in a three-family house in a very nice section of the Bronx. Once during the week, Dad dropped off Jimmy and me so Nana could watch us while he was at work.

Whenever I was thirsty and wanted a drink, Nana gave me a little paper cup filled with water, and when I was finished, I would just throw it in the garbage. One day, she gave me a cup of water, and instead of drinking it right away, I set it on the coffee table. She lived alone, and there was nothing inside of her house to occupy my time, so I was bored inside the house. I asked Nana if I could go outside to burn off some of my energy.

As I was walking out the door, I realized I still hadn't finished my water. I ran over to the table and grabbed the cup of water as Nana loudly shrieked, "No! No!" Guzzling down what I now realized wasn't my water, I regurgitated what I realized was Nana's spit cup. As the smile on Nana's face grew, she told me she had thrown out my water, thinking I no longer wanted it. Nana gave me two cups of water afterward, one to gargle out the slimy, stringy, gooey green mucus and the other to drink. I just used both cups of water to gargle.

Daniel 5:6 (NIV) … "His face turned pale and he was so frightened that his knees knocked together and his legs gave way."

I roamed around outside Nana's house for about ten minutes. I still couldn't get the image of Nana's spit sliding down my throat out of my mind. Having no other remedy in mind, I just grabbed a bunch of green leaves from bushes in front of her house and stuffed them into my mouth, hoping to get that slimy stringy, gooey, green mucus sensation out of my mouth. I decided to go back inside for a drink, hoping I could wash down that sensation inside my mouth.

The first door into the house was the entrance to a small lobby from which you could enter any of the three apartments. I tried to get into the lobby, but the outside door would not open. I would have to ring one of three door bells to get in, but which one should I push? I was frightened about pushing the wrong bell, so I decided to stand outside until someone opened the door.

Psalm 119:176 (NIV) … "I have strayed like a lost sheep. Seek your servant, for I have not forgotten your commands."

I was still standing at the door, looking helpless and in need, when a young man who looked to be about 17 years old approached me and asked, "Are you okay?"

"I'm lost, and I need to get home," I answered. I was too embarrassed to tell him I didn't know which doorbell to ring.

"In what direction do you live?" he asked.

We started to walk toward the direction that I had pointed.

Matthew 5:41 (ESV) ... "And if someone forces you to go one mile, go with him two miles."

After walking about twenty minutes, we came to the intersection of Bruckner Boulevard and Tremont Avenue. I knew that Bruckner Boulevard would lead me home. In the far distance, I could see the twenty-story buildings of the housing projects. We still had about four miles to go.

The teenager couldn't take me all the way, so he flagged down a passing police car. Now I realized I had a big decision to make. After questioning me for about five minutes, the officer figured out that I lived in the Castle Hill Projects.

I wanted to tell the police officer the truth, but I figured even if I did, he wouldn't know which button to push in the tiny lobby of Nana's house. So there I was in the backseat of the police-car on my way to the Castle Hill projects.

Psalm 25:16 (NIV) ... "Turn to me and be gracious to me, for I am lonely and afflicted."

When we arrived back at the projects, I was taken into Building 635 where the administration office was. The police officer left, and there I was, sitting there all alone with a bunch of strange-looking people.

I could hear the voice of a lady talking on the phone in the office. She had called the sanitation department where my dad worked, and she was carefully explaining the situation to someone on the phone. When she finished, she came out of her office and said, "Your dad is on his way to the office from work to take you home."

Job 13:15 (NIV) ... *"Though he slay me, yet will I hope in him; I will surely defend my ways to his face."*

I sat in the office waiting for Dad for about thirty minutes—though it seemed more like hours. I started to think about how mad he was going to be when we got home. I was prepared for a beating, and I imagined how I would cover my head with my arms, and duck to the left and right to avoid the blows from the belt.

Before Dad walked into the office, he paused to give me a long, cold stare. Then he went into the lady's office to sign a paper. He walked out angrily, calling over his shoulder, "Let's go!" Dad didn't say a word as we walked out to the car. I knew he was angry. Dad was standing behind me as I opened the car door to get in, and I was expecting a hard slap to the back of the head, so I quickly dove into the front seat and slammed the door behind me. My foot got caught in the door, and I let out a loud scream. Now I was able to release real tears from the pain and use them as my sympathy theme to divert Dad's attention from my previous charge. Dad didn't flinch, and I now realized big trouble was brewing!

Job 21:27 (NIV) ... *"I know full well what you are thinking, the schemes by which you would wrong me."*

As I wiped my tears, I sat with my head down, buried in my own thoughts, as Dad drove back to our building. Suddenly, my father started to laugh and said, "Okay! What in the world were you thinking?"

Beginning with Nana's spit cup, I explained what happened, and he broke out into uncontrollable laughter. Then I told him about my fear of pushing the wrong doorbell, and that made him laugh even harder. He said he was happy I had gotten him out of work early and that he wasn't having such a good day anyway. We were buddies the rest of the day, watching television and munching snacks. And, I was one happy camper!

Deuteronomy 24:14 (NIV)… "Do not take advantage of a hired worker who is poor and needy, whether that worker is a fellow Israelite or a foreigner residing in one of your towns."

Being the child of a sanitation worker had its rewards. True, we had eight children in the family, and we couldn't afford a lot of things that other families had, but dad got to rummage through other people's garbage all day. He found quite a few interesting souvenirs for our recreational amusement. Better than the souvenirs were the soda bottles buried as treasure in the trash. We would return them to the store and get a few cents for each bottle. Dad would get home around 3:00 p.m., and we would watch from the apartment window as he parked the car on Seward Avenue. If he waved his hand into the air, we knew he had plenty of bottles. We would jump out of the kitchen window and race to the car to claim our bottles. The rule was you could take as many as you could carry.

One day as we were halfway to the store to return our bottles, I tripped and landed on one of my bottles, which exploded under me. As I rolled over the glass, I could feel the pain of a shard ripping into my knee. I quickly sat up and pulled up my pants leg to see a deep gash that was bleeding. As serious as the cut was, no one volunteered to come home with me for fear of losing out on their bottle cash. Dorothy turned into the "Good Samaritan" and took me home. I limped along as I held my hand against the bleeding wound.

Billy and Tommy took all of the bottles into the store for the refunds. Once I got home, Dad tried to stop the bleeding with no success. We needed to go to the doctor's office that was only three blocks away in a private house, displaying a "Doctor's Office" shingle. I wound up getting five stitches into my right knee. That scar also remains to this day.

On the way home, thinking about my portion of the bottles being split up between my siblings upset me. When I limped into the house, I saw much concern on everyone's face about my condition. Then to my complete surprise, all of the money collected from the bottles was on the kitchen table, and I was told it was all mine—a gesture from my siblings for my bravery in allowing the doctor to stitch my knee.

Acts 2:13 (NIV) … "Some, however, made fun of them and said, 'They have had too much wine.' "

As I have already mentioned, Mom was often in the hospital during this time. Then Dad started spending lots of time at a local bar. The Bronx practically had a bar on every street corner. Some days Dad would even take us "barhopping," visiting three or four different bars in the matter of hours. The "Boulevard Bar" was Dad's favorite. He would frequently take us to that particular bar after work.

We would listen to music on the jukebox, bang pool table balls together and play shuffleboard all the while tiptoeing around the drunks, trying to stay out of their way. The bar soon became a normal, very secure and comfortable location to us.

When the drunks in the bar wanted to play shuffleboard, they would bribe us with money, and, in the most arrogant drunk voices, say, "Take this loot and get lost!!"

Whispering, Billy and I would just say, "What schmucks!" as we laughed and bolted out of the door.

Mark 8:36 ... "What good is it for a man to gain the whole world, yet forfeit his soul?"

At times the drunks would give us enough cash to go up the block and around the corner to Frank B.'s toy store. The owner of the store was identical to Ebenezer Scrooge, watching us with a cold, hard stare. Following our every move around the store, he would verbally accuse us of stealing—even before we had the opportunity.

This turned into a mind game with Billy as he would pretend to take an item and put it into his pocket, knowing the owner saw him. Upon leaving the store, Mr. B. would grab Billy and reach into his empty pocket. Disgusted, knowing that Billy had made him look foolish, he would then physically throw us out into the street as we were having a good laugh.

We had times in the bar when our drunken friends would not cooperate in handing over their cash, so we would dupe them out of their money. The way we worked it was quite simple. All of the drunks sat on their barstools with stacks of single dollar bills in front of them with their glasses of beer close by. Billy distracted the drunks, and when their heads turned in his direction, I would swipe a few bucks off their piles.

Billy's favorite diversion was dropping all of the pool balls onto the floor at once, which caused a loud rattling noise as the balls shot off in all directions.

When Dad had his fill of beer, we would all pile into the station wagon for the ride home.

Psalm 18:2 (MSG) ... "God is bedrock under my feet, the castle in which I live, my rescuing knight. My God—the high crag where I run for dear life, hiding behind the boulders, safe in the granite hideout."

Back then, there was no seat belt or DUI law, so we would all pile into the station wagon as we left the bar. As the car would swerve to the left and right, we would be jolted forward and backward collectively. Hollering and laughing, with Dad as the intoxicated ringmaster of entertainment, we would head straight to the Castle—White Castle, that is!

Dad couldn't resist a hamburger after a long day of sloshing down a bunch of beers. In those days, lots of the hamburger joints had waitresses who roller-skated to the window of your car and took your order. There was nothing quite like the sight of a waitress skimming over the sidewalk to your car, while skillfully balancing a tray of food and drinks on one hand.

Gumby's mom worked at White Castle, and it was a treat to see her in her uniform, skating to the car to take our order. When Dad had a few too many beers, we had to endure the embarrassment of Dad slurring his words, while at the same time trying to flirt with Gumby's mom.

Gumby's Mom would smile, give us all a big "Hello," and at the same time politely appease Dad, as he would grovel on and on.

Psalm 139:18 (NIV) … "Were I to count them, they would outnumber the grains of sand. When I awake, I am still with you."

Dad would order thirty or more hamburgers with French fries, and we'd bring them home. Before we could eat, Dad would tell us to put the empty boxes in front of us and count them so we could remember how many hamburgers we were each given.

Billy was busy talking one day, and he lost count of his boxes. That was it for him! He got no more burgers, and I was happy because his remaining portion went right to me. Needless to say, I always kept count!

After our dinner each night, my siblings and I had a chore to do. In the broom closet was a schedule Dad had written out for each daily chore such as cleaning the floor, doing dishes, cleaning bathrooms, etc.

After our fabulous White Castle dinner, Billy had the chore of mopping the floor—the one chore we all tried to avoid. This chore included moving the kitchen table, sweeping the floor, mopping the floor, and returning the table back to its proper place. I was watching Billy as he clowned around placing a sponge under each foot pretending he was ice skating. I saw it coming as Dad turned the corner of the kitchen and caught Billy's clowning act.

As a young man, Dad had been in the Navy, and he taught Billy a lesson Navy style. He had Billy on his knees scrubbing the floor with a toothbrush. As Dad made us watch Billy's punishment, we did all we could not to explode with laughter as tears streamed down my brother's cheeks.

Judges 6:37 (NLT) … "Prove it to me in this way. I will put a wool fleece on the threshing floor tonight. If the fleece is wet with dew in the morning but the ground is dry, then I will know that you are going to help me rescue Israel as you promised."

For most of my childhood, I shared a room and a bed with my brother, Billy who was a real character. He always came up with the most bizarre ideas imaginable. When I was a kid, I would wet the bed, and Dad would get upset because he had to tear the bed apart, then wash the bed sheets and dry out the mattress.

Billy figured out a way to avoid the problem by cutting a hole through the mattress, straight down to the floor, and putting a pan under the bed. He told me to sleep with no underwear, lie on my stomach, and use the hole while I was sleeping, instead of on the bed to avoid punishment for wetting the bed.

I thought his idea was ingenious! To empty the pan in the morning, we would open the bedroom window and toss the "liquid gold" right into the grass.

But, as always, when Dad found out, we both earned the wrong end of the belt buckle.

Genesis 15:12 (NIV) ... "As the sun was setting, Abram fell into a deep sleep, and a thick and dreadful darkness came over him."

With his overactive imagination, Billy seemed to favor inventions and solutions that involved trapdoors and secret openings! There was a point in our childhood when Dad started drinking on the job, and he would come home tipsy, walk into the house, lie down on the couch in the living room, and fall fast asleep.

Billy and I were so skinny, we could easily fit under the couch, in the kitchen cabinets, and even in the oven, which was one of my favorite hiding spots. This fact, combined with my father's habit of taking a mid-afternoon nap, prompted one of Billy's most brilliant ideas!

Matthew 9:16 (NIV) ... "No one sews a patch of unshrunk cloth on an old garment, for the patch will pull away from the garment, making the tear worse."

During one of Billy's adventures of crawling under the couch, he noticed the cloth lining on the underside of the couch. He also noticed that the lining caught items that slipped between the cushions. When Dad took his nap, the loose change in his pockets would fall into the couch lining. If you slid under the couch on your back and looked up into the inner recesses of the couch, you could see the change that had collected in the liner, glinting dimly just beyond your reach.

Billy decided to cut a small hole in the liner so we could reach in with our fingers and pull out the loose change. We could then position ourselves under the couch and simply wait for the change to fall from Dad's pockets while he was off in "Never-Neverland."

Numbers 21:4 (NIV) ... "They traveled from Mount Hor along the route to the Red Sea, to go around Edom. But the people grew impatient on the way."

Still that wasn't enough for Billy! He was impatient with the pace of our financial growth, so he decided to make things move more quickly by ripping out the entire liner. Dad's hard-earned money would then fall straight into our hands.

Once while we waited for the cash to drop into our hands, Dad woke up. He yelled for one of the television "remote controls," which back then was one of the kids, to come and turn on the television to such-and-such channel.

We were stuck under the couch for an hour while he watched his television show. We were underneath the couch, hoping Dad would soon fall asleep so we could make our escape. We realized our future as millionaires would soon be squelched as we could hear our sister, Dorothy, come out of the back bedroom and walk into the bathroom. As Billy and I whispered about Dorothy being in the bathroom, we giggled about how we now had to go to the bathroom ourselves.

Hearing the toilet flush and listening as Dorothy made her way back to the bedroom, we became even more aware of our needing to relieve ourselves. We waited another ten minutes, hoping Dad was now falling asleep.

Suddenly, I felt what I thought was Billy peeing on me, and with a loud whisper, I blistered him for not holding it.

Billy now whispered loudly, "It's not me; it's you!"

Suddenly, we both realized the entire floor under the couch was being flooded. Apparently, the toilet was clogged up and was now overflowing, flooding the hallway, kitchen, and now the living room. We now had no choice but to abandon our position and come out of hiding.

As Billy and I poked our heads from under the couch, at the same time, Dad sat up and put his feet into water that was now up to his ankles. I managed to poke out my head right between Dad's legs as I slipped from under the couch. Billy and I were now sopping wet.

Dad let out a loud screeching holler as he kicked and splashed his legs, bouncing them off our bodies. Stepping over us as he tried to get up from the couch and figure out what was going on, I yelled, "The toilet is overflowing!"

Dad immediately ran to the bathroom and turned the valve to shut off the water. Minutes later, everyone in the house was now on clean-up detail with buckets and mops as Dad took his nap in the back bedroom. By now, the belt buckle across our bodies was something we just expected, and that's what we received a few hours later.

Jeremiah 23:24 (NIV) … "Who can hide in secret places so that I cannot see them?" declares the LORD. *"Do not I fill heaven and earth?" declares the* LORD.

Ever since the caveman came up with the idea of hiding in caves, the famous and favorite "Hide and Seek," was a natural for Billy and me because of the suspenseful nature of the unknown. Our apartment was very large, and we were still tiny, so we could hide anywhere for hours and never be found.

One day I spent two hours looking for Billy, looking in every great hiding spot I knew. Finally, he walked in the front door laughing. He snickered, " I got bored, so I thought it would be fun to go outside while you were searching for me in the house."

I was furious, and within seconds, I began plotting my revenge! What he had done was clearly a breach of the rules of the game. So I waited and let some time pass, knowing he had forgotten about his prank before I pulled the same stunt. Billy hid, and I left him hiding for a couple of hours while I hung outside with friends.

My revenge indeed was sweet. But an even better revenge was after a long day of burning energy down near the second mountain. I must have eaten a ton of wild blackberries. That night as we slept in bed together, my rear exploded with diarrhea all over his body. He cried like a baby, and I laughed like a hyena.

Psalm 104:4 (NIV) ... "He makes winds his messengers, flames of fire his servants."

All of the buildings in the projects had incinerators to burn garbage. On each floor in the hallway, there was a square metal plate with a handle. You would simply pull the handle toward you and slide your garbage down the open chute. The garbage would fall into the incinerator, and the maintenance workers would burn the garbage every day, usually in the morning.

From the first floor, we could open the plate door and see the intense flames from the burning garbage. One maintenance worker named Jose would always jokingly chase me around the lobby and threaten to throw me into the fire. When he did finally catch me, he would pick me up, take me over to the incinerator, open it so I could see the flames and feel the intense heat. I would kick and scream, and become panicked to the delight of onlookers, including all my friends and family. When the fun was over, Jose would put me down, hand me some change from his pocket, and I would have the last laugh, knowing if I played this game there was some money in it for me.

Mom walked into the house one day after dumping our garbage into the incinerator. She was shaking and crying hysterically. Apparently being as skinny as she was, her wedding band slipped off her finger and ended up in the bottom of the incinerator, along with the rest of the garbage. Hoping Dad would console and comfort her, just the opposite happened. Dad screamed and belittled Mom as if she were a kid. After his explosion she was sent to her room to think about what she had done.

Joshua 10:9 (NIV) ... "After an all-night march from Gilgal, Joshua took them by surprise."

One would think, after such trauma, I would fear the incinerator. The police in our neighborhood handed out tickets for ridiculous petty crimes like walking on the grass and loitering in the lobby. We would always run away as fast as we could if we saw a police officer while walking on the grass or loitering. If we did get a ticket, it usually meant a fine of a few dollars that our parents would have to pay!

One day, Billy and I saw some big cardboard boxes in the back of our building where oversized garbage (such as furniture and beddings) was thrown out. We decided to take the boxes and stuff them half in and half out of the incinerator and set fire to them, watching as the intense flames would shoot into the lobby.

Of course, I was sent back into our house to mischievously find the matches, knowing that to be captured was sure doom. When I got back, Billy was waiting impatiently having the cardboard boxes in place ready for the flame. We were excitedly engaged in our arsonist activities when the staircase door flew open. The door banged loudly against the wall, echoing throughout the hallway, scaring the daylights out of us. As we jumped back from the incinerator, a policeman came storming out of the stairway with his nightstick in hand!

1 John 1:6 (NIV) ... "If we claim to have fellowship with him and yet walk in the darkness, we lie and do not live out the truth."

Billy instantly took off running and was able to escape, but not before the police officer started yelling for him to stop. Then he flung his nightstick at Billy, hitting his ankle. Billy just kept running. When I tried to run, the officer grabbed me by my collar and proceeded to drag me to where the nightstick had made its final landing. He was upset that Billy was able to get away. Then he picked up the nightstick and gave me a hard whack across my butt.

He viciously asked, "What's the name of the boy who ran away?"

My mind raced, thinking about the punishment I would get from Dad if he found out what we had been planning to do. I lied and answered, "It was Scott—a new guy I met today."

"I'm giving you a ticket. What's your name?"

I lied again, saying, "My name's Tommy C." "Where do you live?"

I lied a third time and gave Tommy C.'s apartment number—12-G.

I knew my quick thinking would keep me out of trouble because the policeman would never know who I was. However, I didn't bargain for the long arm of the law!

2 Peter 2:9 (ESV) ... "Then the Lord knows how to rescue the godly from trials, and to keep the unrighteous under punishment until the day of judgment."

About one hour later, I was in the C.'s apartment on the twelfth floor, hanging out in the back bedroom with Tommy C. when I heard a loud knock on the front door. Mr. C. answered the door and my "friend," Mr. Police Officer, was standing there. Mr. C. and the officer talked for a few minutes, and I knew exactly what they were talking about.

After handing Mr C. a ticket for the offense, the officer left. Mr. C. screamed at the top of his lungs for Tommy to get out from the backroom and into the living room. "Tommy, why were you burning cardboard near the incinerator? Who was the other kid who took off running?"

Exodus 23:7 (NIV) … "Have nothing to do with a false charge and do not put an innocent or honest person to death, for I will not acquit the guilty."

Tommy C. just stood dumbfounded, looking at his father. "It wasn't me," he declared, but his father would not believe him.

His father gave him several chances to admit to his crime, but Tommy kept insisting it wasn't him. I thought my father gave the worst beatings in the world until I saw Tommy's father beating him.

I stood watching Tommy get beat, knowing I was the guilty one who should have been receiving the beating, but I couldn't say a word or move. I was just frozen in my place with fear running throughout my little body. Tommy was being punished after his beating, so I had to leave. I went downstairs and roamed around outside the building, thinking about my narrow escape.

Luke 6:33 (NIV)… "And if you do good to those who are good to you, what credit is that to you? Even sinners do that."

When I got outside of the building, Frankie was there. Frankie lived on the fifth floor, but we never spent much time together because he had tough restrictions on his curfew—unlike our family where there was a chain of command. Older brothers and sisters were in charge of the whereabouts of the younger ones. Basically, that meant I was free to stay out all day as long as I made it home for dinner at 5:00 p.m. After dinner, we were permitted to go back outside until the streetlights came on. Of course I broke that rule almost every night because my older siblings were also outside until 9:00 p.m., and they were in charge.

Seeing my options were low in the friend department that day, and there was no one else outside but Frankie, I agreed to a game of catch using his softball. Frankie's father always accompanied Frankie wherever he went, and it was fairly uncomfortable having his father breathing down my neck and watching everything I did. Frankie's dad knew I was in trouble more often than not, so he watched me like a hawk.

After about fifteen minutes of tossing the softball, Frankie started acting tough, showing off in front of his dad. I told Frankie's dad, hoping he would intervene, but his dad wanted us to get into a fight because he figured Frankie could whip me.

James 4:1 (NIV)… "What causes fights and quarrels among you? Don't they come from your desires that battle within you?"

The time had come, I couldn't take it anymore. Frankie just crossed the line by calling me a "scaredy-cat". I jumped on him and started pounding him. His dad stood there, cheering his son on, yelling, "Take charge! Whip him." To make matters worse, a gathering crowd formed along with Frankie's little brother who was right by his side, screaming at the top of his lungs for him to kick my butt.

Frankie was an awkward kid, and he didn't fight very much or know how to. I was giving him a kid beating, and after a few minutes, I had him pinned to the ground. I was just about to punch him in the face when, out of the corner of my eye, I saw Frankie's dad staring hard at me with a stern look on his face that terrified me.

With my arm up in the air and my fist clenched, I felt as if I was in a freeze frame. Poised to beat Frankie into submission, I don't know if it was some kind of magical compassion or just the fear of that stern look Frankie's dad gave me. I made a split-second decision to stop.

1 Chronicles 16:9 (NIV) ... "Sing to him, sing praise to him; tell of all his wonderful acts."

I dropped my arm, stood up, and helped Frankie to his feet and even brushed him off. "Frankie, I don't want to fight you."

What happened next took me by total surprise and left me in shock. Frankie's dad came over to me, shook my hand, praised me for not pounding Frankie senseless when I had the chance, and for helping him up. He praised my virtue. "Great kid!"

I was embarrassed. I had only let Frankie up because I was scared of his dad. I knew that if his dad had not been there, things would have ended differently. Frankie's dad invited me up to their apartment for a lunch fit for a king and to watch Saturday morning television. I was stunned again! I had never been inside Frankie's apartment before, and I was amazed at the number of action figures and miniature sport cars he had. But the possession that impressed me the most was their beautiful full-size color television.

Genesis 9:16 (NIV) ... "Whenever the rainbow appears in the clouds, I will see it and remember the everlasting covenant between God and all living creatures of every kind on the earth."

This was the first time I had ever seen a color television. I just sat in awe, trying to comprehend all the magnificence of the screen in front of me. Oh, sure, we had all heard the hype about color televisions from my dad, and we figured we would eventually get one. But never had I expected it would look as spectacular as it did!

When the long-awaited day came, and we got our first color television, everyone was excited. On the day the television was to be delivered, we waited anxiously, hoping it would arrive early in the day. The movie "The Wizard of Oz" was going to be aired that evening, and we had heard through the grapevine that, when the house dropped into the Land of Oz landing on that old wicked witch, and Dorothy opened the door, everything turned from black-and-white to color.

We watched from our window as the delivery truck pulled up to Seward Avenue. As the deliverymen were unloading the gigantic box containing our color television, we exploded from our kitchen window, jumping into the grass and running up the hill. We ran out to the street, hoping to help them carry the huge box into the house but they wouldn't let us. We did open the doors and directed them down the hallway to our front door.

Billy jokingly grabbed a broom from the broom closet and walked in front of the delivery men, sweeping an imaginary path all the way into the house, treating the men as royalty. When the men left, we stood in the living room having a ceremony connecting the antenna which, at the time, we called "rabbit ears." We were able to watch "The Wizard of Oz" in brilliant Technicolor for the first time. It definitely lived up to all the hype.

As Frankie and I continued hanging out that day in his room, I asked, "Can you open a window? It's hot in here."

"The windows are locked and will only open about six inches."

"That's fine. By the way, I should probably run downstairs to my apartment and let someone know where I am."

I walked out of the room and down the hall where his dad was in the kitchen. "Where are you going?" he asked, so I explained what I had told Frankie. With a big smile, he responded, "Hurry back, pal!"

When I got out of that apartment, I was excited. I ran to the stairway door and began jumping two steps at a time all the way to the first floor. I ran as fast as I could to our apartment door and running inside, I shouted Billy's name as loud as possible. "Billy! Billy!" I frantically searched each room, but he was nowhere to be found. I bolted out the door straight up to Gumby's house with no luck.

Deciding to try our house again, I went to the first floor and was rushing down the hall when I thought he might be looking for junk out back on the side of the building. Sure enough, there he was on top of an old discarded couch, balancing himself as if on a tightrope. I told him what had happened with Frankie, and he got as excited as I did about what I was planning.

We were both laughing as Billy stormed out the front building exit and positioned himself right below Frankie's window. I took the elevator back up to Frankie's apartment and knocked on the door. "Welcome back, my friend!" Frankie's dad shouted as I made my way down the hall to the bedroom. After about five minutes, I asked Frankie if he could get me a glass of water, and he replied, "Sure, Buddy." As soon as he left the room, I grabbed a G.I. Joe action figure along with a bunch of Hot Wheel miniature racecars, ran to the open window, and tossed the items out to where Billy was waiting below to scoop them up. I sent him on quite a few more errands in the next fifteen minutes, and each time he left the room, I found a few more items to toss out of the window.

The next time I saw Frankie and his dad, I happily greeted them with a big hello. All I received in return was cold, hard stares. After that day, I was never again invited into Frankie's house.

Exodus 3:2 (NIV) … "There the angel of the LORD appeared to him in flames of fire from within a bush. Moses saw that though the bush was on fire it did not burn up."

My brother, Billy, introduced me to Robbie G., better known as the kid with the flaming red hair and freckles. This new friend was the same age as Billy and Gumby—three years older than me. Robbie would roam the streets with his eyes focused on the street curbs or walk around the neighborhood with his head down looking for discarded cigarettes in the street. If the cigarette he found had been smoked only halfway, Robbie would pick it up, light it up and smoke the rest of the cigarette. I thought this was disgusting, and Billy agreed.

Robbie was the first person I knew who was a hunter. Each year, Mr. G. would take Robbie hunting for deer in upstate New York. Every year when they arrived back from their hunting trip, Billy and I would stand behind their car, staring at a freshly shot deer strapped to the roof of their car.

Robbie's mom had a special whistling sound she was able to make by sucking wind into her mouth. When it was time for Robbie to come home, she would open their tenth-floor window that faced the mountains side of the building, stick her head halfway out the window and let loose. Everyone in the building knew Mrs. G.'s whistle—a loud, high-pitched sound that could be heard anywhere near our building. Kids, as well as adults, tried in vain to imitate that whistle without success. It was known as Mrs. G.'s whistle.

One day as I was looking out of my bedroom window, I saw Robbie and Billy on their knees in the street, looking down at something. I looked at the deer strapped to the back of the G.'s car and then back at them on their knees. I looked back at the deer, then back at them, then back at the deer. This repetition went on for about two minutes as I was trying to make a connection between the deer and their being on their knees, looking toward the ground. Finally, curiosity got the best of me, and I leaped out of my bedroom window and ran as fast as I could through the grass and up the hill to see what they were doing.

When I got there, both Billy and Robbie were now on their stomachs looking down the street sewer. They each had a long tree branch reaching down to the bottom of the sewer, trying to retrieve a crunched-up pack of cigarettes someone had thrown or dropped into the sewer.

Matthew 15:17 (NLT) … "Anything you eat passes through the stomach and then goes into the sewer."

As they were struggling and squirming on their stomachs, each holding their sticks and trying to grab one end of the crunched cigarette pack to haul it to the surface, I got down on my stomach and watched as it turned into a game of who could hold on the longest to get the cigarette pack to the surface without dropping it. As I was down on my stomach, trying to get a better view at how each was performing, I noticed my head was able to fit into the sewer opening.

The sewer opening was against the street curb, and before I knew it, I had my chest and head halfway into the sewer, peering down at the pack of cigarettes. I pulled my head out and excitedly stood, telling Billy and Robbie that I could fit down the sewer!

They dropped their sticks, and together jumped to their feet, then shouted "Hallelujah!" We all agreed I was going down into the sewer, feet first and backward. As they held me, I slowly was let down to metal bars against the side of the sewer wall that formed a ladder. As scary as it was, the adrenalin was pumping so fast, I overcame the fear of the unknown.

Haggai 2:8 (ESV) ... "The silver is mine, and the gold is mine, declares the LORD of hosts."

As I slowly made my way down to the bottom of the sewer, I was taking it one slow step at a time. The ladder bars ended, leaving a few feet for me to jump down to the ground. After jumping the rest of the way, I slipped on a thin coat of dark-black mud that covered the sewer surface, gashing my knees and landing on my stomach.

Billy and Robbie were screaming down at me. "What else is down there?"

As I slowly stood up on the slippery surface, trying to get my balance, I looked around and noticed a whole bunch of items that we could not see from street level. The first thing I noticed was some loose change—about twelve cents. I picked it up and put it right into my pocket. I grabbed the cigarette pack, that had about seven cigarettes in it and put it in my other pocket.

Billy suddenly yelled, "A cop is coming! We'll come back after he passes by. Keep quiet!"

As I looked around, I realized I was now living with the big, fat sewer rats, and the sewer smell was becoming overwhelming as if a skunk had been there. I had to cover my nose and try to breathe only through my mouth.

I picked up a few Spaulding balls used for playing stickball. I then noticed a cigarette lighter and a stickball bat. I was on a roll, thinking, "I've found a gold mine!"

But then I started to get nervous because it had been a while since Billy and Robbie had left. I figured it was time to get out of there, and I tried to jump up to the first rung of the ladder with no luck. I was now starting to freak out, thinking I wasn't going to be able to get out of the sewer, and that sooner or later, a bunch of hungry rats would show up.

Billy and Robbie finally returned, and yelled into the sewer at me. "What else did you find?"

Instead of telling them what I had found, I told them my situation about jumping to the first step. They encouraged me and assured me that I could do it. Five jumps later, I finally made it, barely holding on to the first step. After struggling to the top of the steps, I now had to slide my head back out of a tight squeeze with the rest of my body following.

When my head was sticking out of the sewer, both Billy and Robbie grabbed me by the neck and pulled my body the rest of the way out of the sewer. When I was finally on the ground, Billy and Robbie began treating me like royalty. We spent the rest of the day with my climbing down sewers, looking for more treasures. Searching sewers became a ritual several times a week.

GOOSE BUMPS

▲ ▲ ▲

JOHN 7:49 (NIV) … "No! But this mob that knows nothing of the law— there is a curse on them."

Tommy, who was nicknamed "Worm" because he could slither his way in and out of any tight spot, was an older brother to Billy and me. One day, as we were enjoying the afternoon watching television with Dad, we heard a loud rumbling sound echoing off the walls of the hallway just outside our door. It sounded like a runaway train.

Suddenly, the front door blew open, and Tommy came running into the apartment, gasping for air. Sweat was pouring down his face.

Dad, in his "what-in-the-world-is-going-on" voice, asked why he had bolted into the house that way and what the booming sound was.

"Ten or more guys outside chased me from the park. They want to smash my face in. These guys always chase me, and so far, I have always been able to outrun them."

Right then and there, Dad gave him a choice to make. "Tommy, go out in the hallway and stand up to all of them, or take a beating from me."

Tommy thought Dad was kidding and started to walk down the hall to his room when Dad yelled even louder, "THEM OR ME?"

Tommy looked back at Dad with an expression on his face that said "Are you really serious?" Tommy was scared to death, but when faced with the choice of standing up to them or taking a beating from Dad, he chose standing up to the guys in the hallway.

Psalm 112:7 (NASB) … "He will not fear evil tidings; His heart is steadfast, trusting in the LORD."

Once his knees stopped shaking, Tommy walked straight out the door. You could have cut the tension with a knife now. I felt courageous for the moment, thinking that Dad was coming with us. I had visions of Dad's twirling six or seven guys over his shoulders into the grass until he mentioned the little fact that we were on our own.

We could see the fear in Tommy's face as the gang of guys all began to race toward him like a pack of wolves, swarming around him chanting, "Worm, Worm, Worm."

If not for the fact of knowing the consequences we would had received from Dad, Billy and I would have run away as fast as we could. But Tommy stood his ground with both fists raised.

Suddenly, all the guys stopped and looked at Tommy. Then one bewildered boy asked, "Aren't you going to run?"

"No!" Tommy said, "I'll fight all of you."

As a group, the boys turned, snickering with disappointment as they walked away. Tommy stared at them in disbelief. As they were leaving, one of the guys said simply, "We just enjoyed chasing you."

I'm not sure what lesson Tommy learned from that encounter, but I know that facing the boys he feared gave him some confidence.

Revelation 6:13 (NIV) … "and the stars in the sky fell to earth, as figs drop from a fig tree when shaken by a strong wind."

One of our childhood heroes was Johnny Weissmuller who starred as Tarzan, the ape man, in the 1930s and 1940s movies. Imitating Tarzan's swinging from the trees and yodeling the Tarzan yell, the three mountain area became our jungle.

Once while swinging from tree to tree with the C. brothers, Gumby and a few other guys, James C. also known as "Bone," decide to really test his swinging ability. Standing on a thick tree branch measuring a jump to another thick tree branch on the next tree, he planned to use a vine branch that was hanging from the top of the other tree to swing across the two thick branches safely. The distance between the trees was about ten feet, and the drop below was about the same distance.

While Bone was in the tree, everyone else was on the ground looking up at him. Half of us were yelling to go ahead and try the daredevil stunt while the other half shouted up advice from below not to do it, convinced he would never make the distance.

Bone stood on the tree limb for about ten minutes, debating and drumming up the courage to take the leap. Letting out his best Tarzan yodel, he leaped off the branch and hanging onto the vine, he swished through the air. Both feet landed safely on his targeted branch.

With a sigh of relief from all the guys below, Bone let go of the vine. While standing on the tree branch, thinking all was well, he lost his balance. Then he began a slow descent backward to the earth. All that could now be heard was gasping from the silent jungle as we helplessly watched.

A big brick was positioned right below the tree, and within moments, the back of Bone's head was going to come in contact with it.

The next sound we heard was a loud "THUMP." As Bone laid lifeless on the ground, his brother, Eddie, ran to his side and knelt down next to him. Eddie placed his hand under Bone's head and lifted him into a sitting position.

As Bone's eyes started to open, so did his mouth—pouring out profanities. Eddie then noticed the thick red blood that was oozing from the back of Bone's head. Gumby jumped right into action. He dropped to the ground, pulling off his sneakers and socks. Taking his socks, he immediately covered the deep gash on Bone's head. All of us moved as one unit as quickly as we could in the direction of our building. At the same time, we applied Gumby's socks to the back of Bone's head.

We listened as Bone squealed about feeling light-headed. Eight stitches later, we all received a scolding education from the doctor on how we unintentionally did the wrong thing by placing a dirty pair of blue socks on Bone's head. "The dye from the socks could have seeped into his brain and killed him," he explained.

Job 37:6 (NASB) … "For to the snow He says, 'Fall on the earth,' And to the downpour and the rain, 'Be strong.' "

One winter, we experienced a blizzard that left more than a foot of snow on the ground. Brothers Tommy and Michael, along with George C., and a few other guys, including myself, trudged through the snow to the mountains. We spent hours horse playing around, courageously jumping off the mountains into the deep-white, crystal, powder-puff snow banks. As time quickly passed and we started back home, a bragging rights contest ensued on who could make it back to the building first.

That challenge began an all-out brawl of pushing, shoving and pulling each other into the snow, trying to stop one another from winning the contest. As our family gathered around the dinner table, Dad noticed Michael was missing from the crew and asked if anyone had seen him. Each head waggled back and forth in turn answering "No." None of us had seen him.

Dad got on the phone and called Mr. C. to ask if Michael was upstairs with George, but Mr. C. said Michael wasn't there. Mr. C. asked George if he knew where Michael could be. George said Michael had gone to the second mountain, and that he remembered Michael's jumping off the high part of the mountain. He didn't remember Michael being a part of the wild race home with the rest of the guys. Tommy had no clue where Michael was because he was preoccupied with the fact that he had won the wild race home and was consumed with his own greatness.

So, my Dad, Mr. C., and all of the crew from both families set out as a search party, going to the second mountain to look for Michael.

Proverbs 7:9 (NIV) ... *"At twilight, as the day was fading, as the dark of night set in."*

It was dark by now, and as our mob frantically searched with flashlights and candles, my heart was pounding in my chest because it was spooky-dark and scary. We searched in unbearable silence with only the sound of crunching snow under our feet. A faint, dark, cold wind accompanied our periodic cries of "Michael! Michael!"

With time passing, and Dad's realizing Michael must be somewhere else, he decided it was time to call off the search. As we started to leave, someone heard a faint cry in the snow below the second mountain. "Everyone! Be quiet!" Dad ordered. As we listened closely, we could hear a faint whimper but couldn't locate the source.

When Dad yelled out for Michael, we could hear a cry. As he began shining his flashlight in the direction of the voice toward the mountain, we saw Michael stuck in snow up to his chest. We dug him out and carried him home, like a giant popsicle stick from the neighborhood ice cream truck.

Once he was home safely and wrapped in warm blankets, Michael was surprisingly fine and seemed no worse for the experience. Nonetheless, the search took a toll on the rest of us. Nobody wanted to think about what might have happened if we hadn't heard the faint whimper.

Proverbs 12:26 (NASB) … "The righteous is a guide to his neighbor, But the way of the wicked leads them astray."

The T. family lived directly across from our building in building number 2140. Their eldest son, Steven, had the nickname "Rico." Two other boys were in their family, Tommy and Dennis (the youngest of the siblings, at that time, because within the next few years Mrs. T. would give birth to a few more boys). Priscilla, the only girl, was the oldest child. My brother, Jimmy, and Dennis T. would stay together every now and then, while Billy and I connected with Rico and Tommy.

One evening, while we were having dinner, Dad received a call from Mr. T., asking if Dennis was in our house or if we knew where Dennis might be.

After quizzing us, Dad told Mr. T. that we had no idea where Dennis was, and we continued with our dinner.

1 Peter 3:16 (NASB) … "and keep a good conscience so that in the thing in which you are slandered, those who revile your good behavior in Christ will be put to shame."

Around the dinner table, we were in deep conversation about the activities of the day when my brother, Jimmy, let out a little sniffle, then another little sniffle. Suddenly, like an exploding stick of dynamite, he busted out wailing hysterically and started to cry uncontrollably. The tears ran down his cheeks like a flowing river.

We laughed and mocked him, as brothers will do, but Dad told us to stop laughing, and he solemnly asked, "Jimmy, what's wrong?"

My thinking was he didn't like the meatloaf and was afraid to tell Dad. It took Jimmy some time to calm down enough to tell us the story.

"Dennis and I were playing down at the mountains today. Dennis found a large locker cabinet that was thrown out as garbage. Dennis told me to get inside it, and he would close it on me. I didn't want to get inside, so Dennis said he would get inside, and I could close the door. Dennis squeezed into the locker, and I shut the door.

"After a few minutes, Dennis told me to open the door, but I couldn't get it open. It was locked! Dennis started to scream at me. He told me if I didn't open the locker right then, he would do me bodily harm. I tried to open the locker, but I couldn't."

Apparently Jimmy started backing up as he listened to the screams from Dennis become fainter and fainter. Finally Jimmy turned and ran full-speed toward home, leaving Dennis inside the locker.

Mark 14:50 (NASB) ... "And they all left Him and fled."

We were astonished and couldn't believe what we were hearing. Dennis was all alone near the mountains—in the dark and stuck in a locker. And our brother, Jimmy, had left him there?

Dad called Mr. T. back to explain what had happened, and once again, the Murrays were about to become part of a search-and-rescue party. Our family joined the entire T. clan, marching to the mountains with flashlights and candles, hoping Dennis was not hurt or injured. This time, we knew exactly where to find the lost boy.

Billy and I couldn't stop laughing under our breath at the thought of seeing Dennis' face all alone in that locker. When we approached the locker, we could here Dennis crying faintly. Mr. T. called out to him, asking, "Are you all right?"

Dennis replied that he was, though he sounded frightened.

When we finally got the locker open, Dennis jumped out and immediately ran after Jimmy screaming wildly, "You're dead!"

Jimmy made it safely home in record time—before Dennis could catch him.

2 Samuel 12:23 (AMPC)… "But now he is dead; why should I fast? Can I bring him back again? I shall go to him, but he will not return to me."

Jimmy had not had his last brush with heart-pounding dread. I was sitting in my room one day when Jimmy came in looking as if he had seen a ghost. When I asked him what was wrong, he said, "A friend and I were down near the mountains, and we found…uh…something.

"What was it?"

"Uh, I'm not sure…either a toy doll or a dead baby."

We sat in my room for a while as I interrogated him, thinking it was a doll and that he had simply let his imagination run away with him. The only other person home at the time was my sister, Alice, so I finally said, "We had better tell Alice about what you found."

Alice said we had to call the police because Jimmy seemed fairly sure that what he had found was, in fact, a dead baby.

The police came to the apartment and questioned Jimmy. Then I went with Alice and Jimmy to the police car, and we headed toward the mountains. Jimmy took us to the spot, and sure enough, there was a baby wrapped in a blood-stained brown paper bag, and it was dead.

Jimmy and I could not comprehend what had happened or how this baby had died. Alice tried to delicately explain the concept of abortion.

Death was something I couldn't yet understand, but I knew it was real. That experience of finding the baby somehow changed me.

Matthew 19:14 (ESV) ... "But Jesus said, 'Let the little children come to me and do not hinder them, for to such belongs the kingdom of heaven.' "

Our friend, Carmine, lived in the private houses down the block from our building. He was a good kid, who was very funny. Billy, Carmine, and I were rolling around inside a big cardboard box in front of Carmine's house one day. After a few hours, Billy and I decided to head back to the projects, letting Carmine know that we would see him the next day.

My dad worked late that night, and Billy and I were outside fooling around in the grass when he arrived home. Dad went into the house, and about 15 minutes later, he called from the kitchen window, asking us to come into the apartment. When we got inside, Dad asked us to sit down. He had a very serious look on his face as he asked us if we had been playing with Carmine earlier in the day.

Not knowing which answer would keep us out of trouble, we told the truth. We told him we had. He said that Carmine had continued playing in the cardboard box after we had left him, and that he was crushed to death by the back wheels of a sanitation truck.

1 Samuel 20:32 (NIV) ... " 'Why should he be put to death? What has he done?' Jonathan asked his father."

The sanitation driver had backed his truck onto the box, not knowing that Carmine was inside. Dad told us that the driver was a friend of his, and that they had taken the driver to the hospital because he needed help from a mental health doctor.

When Dad told us that Carmine was dead, we couldn't believe what we were hearing. I stared, dumbstruck, at my father as he tried to warn us against playing in cardboard boxes. I had no words to describe how I felt on that day, nor could I answer the questions that came into my head.

Death was a great, black abyss yawning wide before me, and I didn't know how to protect myself, or anyone, for that matter, from its clutches. It seemed random and cruel. As I listened to my dad droning on about the great danger of cardboard boxes, I wondered to myself if Carmine knew he was dead.

For months after that event, whenever I saw a large cardboard box, I wouldn't go near it. Panic would fill my body along with images of Carmine inside the box being crushed to death.

Job 22:12 (NIV) ... "Is not God in the heights of heaven? And see how lofty are the highest stars!"

Carmine's death wasn't the last time I would come face-to-face with the "Grim Reaper." The day was like any other in the projects, that is until a crowd started to gather outside of our building. Everyone was buzzing, and a palpable tension filled the air—as if someone had turned on an electrical current.

I walked toward the crowd, asking everyone along the way what was going on. Someone responded in a sad voice saying, "The nice old lady who lived on the ninth floor jumped out of the window and killed herself." A neighbor had politely covered her with a blanket, but I could see the blood seeping into the grass beneath her body. I stood among the onlookers, feeling helpless. I thought of her seated on a bench in the small park in front of our building, talking with the other elders, enjoying their company. Occasionally, they would scold us for making noise, running too fast, or some other perceived violation.

Being boys, we would try to think of new ways to annoy them. Now that she was dead, I considered if I should feel sorry about my annoying her, but that thought was pushed aside by my concern regarding the "why" of the whole thing. "Why would she jump out of a window to her death? Why would anyone, for that matter? What did she think about before she jumped?" These questions and others like them plagued me. I would witness for years to come many others commit suicide from the rooftops.

Proverbs 17:25 (ESV) ... "A foolish son is a grief to his father and bitterness to her who bore him."

Brian was Billy's age, and he lived down the hall from our apartment. Probably because he had three much older brothers, Brian always seemed to know more about the tricks of life than many of us guys. When he would speak, it was always with a commanding authority, and his voice always rang with the distinctive sound of the truth with confidence.

Brian made dummies out of old clothes stuffed with newspapers. The dummies were about five feet in height, and if you looked quickly from a distance, his dummy appeared to be a real person. We thought his invention had some real potential for some high-strung pranks. When a person walked into the hallway, they would think we were beating and stomping on someone and try to stop us. Of course, our high jinks left the person feeling dumber than the dummy.

Our "victims" would get pretty angry when they realized we were only kicking around a bunch of clothing stuffed with paper.

Some would chase us all around the building, up and down the staircases, huffing and puffing, as doors swung open, slamming against the wall and then slamming shut, making booming sounds throughout the building. We would normally outrun the victims we had made fools of.

Once as I was being chased by one guy, I mistakenly ran outside to the front of our building. Our building had three different entrances, and each time I would sneak around to get back into one of those entrances, he would be standing there smiling and laughing. Finally, I gave up and climbed into our back bedroom window and made my escape.

The next day, the gang told me that the guy had stayed in the lobby for about an hour. He was checking every entrance to make sure I couldn't get back into the building. The gang sat on the dummy against the mailboxes, laughing hysterically knowing that I had climbed into my window.

Meanwhile, this guy had no clue that I lived on the first floor, and eventually, he gave up while swearing and mumbling a few profanities, then stormed angrily into the elevator.

Proverbs 24:28 (ESV) … "Be not a witness against your neighbor without cause, and do not deceive with your lips."

Whenever my brother, Billy, got together with Brian, there was bound to be trouble! They both suffered from imagination overdrive! One day, Billy was looking out of the lobby window at the old people sitting in the park on a bench. He decided it would be fun to play the same prank on them.

"Get in a circle and start beating on one of Brian's dummies. We can watch them get excited and start screaming at us to stop," he proposed.

Brian agreed with the plan, but he felt his idea had more zing to it. Brian said that I should go outside with a few of the other guys and sit on the bench next to the old people. Then Billy and Brian would take the elevator to the twelfth floor. From the twelfth floor, they would take the stairs up to the roof, where they would pretend to be fighting and struggling with one another on the roof top. Those of us on the ground would look up at the roof and start pointing up to get the attention of the old people. He told us to start hollering about the guys fighting on the roof.

When everyone was watching the fake fight, Brian would grab the dummy and throw it off the roof. The old people would think it was a real person. As the dummy hit the ground, we would laugh. The old folks would gasp, thinking they had witnessed a tragic event. We would then grab the dummy and run away to play the same prank on others in different buildings throughout the projects. No doubt we would have some hilarious moments throughout the day!

"P.S. 138"

▲ ▲ ▲

PROVERBS 22:3 (NIV) … "THE prudent see danger and take refuge, but the simple keep going and pay the penalty."

If you have ever lived in New York City, I don't have to tell you about the Mr. Softee Ice Cream truck. Some of you might know about the Good Humor truck, but in our neighborhood, it was always Mr. Softee! The truck would pull up on Seward Avenue, directly in front of our windows, around the same time every day, with bells blasting and kids running like excited tail-wagging dogs.

Kids would swarm the truck for ice cream cones and popsicles, waving at the driver and dropping nickels and dimes around the truck tires as they dug in their pockets for change. Most of the time, we couldn't buy ice cream because we didn't have the extra money, but we still would run over to the ice cream truck and put on our sad-sack faces, hoping someone would buy us a cone.

The ice cream wasn't the only reason we hastily ran to the Softee truck. We would wait until everyone had bought their ice cream, and the driver was about to leave. As the driver was about to pull away, we would jump on the back of his truck for a ride to the traffic light at Castle Hill Avenue.

Billy had the idea that it would be fun to tie Brian's dummy to the back of the ice cream truck and watch it get dragged up the block. While the other kids were buying their goodies, Billy tied the dummy to the back of the truck, and we waited in anticipation for the ice cream man to pull out.

Ecclesiastes 3:4 (NIV) ... "a time to weep and a time to laugh, a time to mourn and a time to dance."

As the truck started to move, we chased it up the block. Billy was laughing uncontrollably as he ran behind the truck, trying to catch up with our runaway dummy. Without warning, Billy jumped onto the belly of the dummy landing upright on both knees, riding atop the stuffed fabric with an insane look in his eyes.

We stopped running and just stood there laughing hysterically, watching as Billy and the dummy were dragged off behind the truck. The truck headed up Seward Avenue toward Castle Hill Avenue, traveling about thirty miles an hour. The driver didn't know he had "passengers," and he kept increasing his speed as we watched, now holding our breath and hoping for the best.

Acts 17:28 (NLT) ... "For in him we live and move and exist. As some of your own poets have said, 'We are his offspring.'"

Billy seemed oblivious to what was going on. He was absolutely having a ball! Normally the driver would stop at the red light on the corner, but today the light stayed green, and he kept speeding toward the intersection. He was going to make a left onto Castle Hill Avenue when the light turned from green to yellow and then to red. This was Billy's chance to hop off before he really got hurt. However, the driver must have been in a rush because he speeded up and sailed right through the traffic light just as it turned yellow.

We weren't laughing anymore because we knew Billy could get hurt. Unfortunately, there was nothing we could do but stand there and watch!

Genesis 39:15 (NIV) … "When he heard me scream for help, he left his cloak beside me and ran out of the house."

The truck was now traveling about 40 miles an hour as it came out of the turn and accelerated on the wide strip of Castle Hill Ave. Now we could hear Billy screaming and see him clinging onto the disintegrating dummy for dear life. As the driver came out of the turn, the tension on the rope increased, and it could no longer support Billy's weight. The rope snapped, and Billy and the dummy kept going straight through the intersection as the ice cream truck completed the left turn and continued up Castle Hill Avenue. Billy managed to stay on the dummy for about fifteen feet, and then he lost his grip. The dummy flew off in one direction while Billy tumbled in the opposite direction.

Acts 19:32 (NIV) … "The assembly was in confusion: Some were shouting one thing, some another. Most of the people did not even know why they were there."

The cars in the intersection slammed on their brakes to avoid hitting Billy and his stuffed friend. We took off running up the street toward Billy as he kept sliding another ten feet or so and finally came to a stop.

I ran toward my brother. My heart was pumping fast, hoping he was not hurt badly, and hoping he wasn't dead. As we were running, I heard Brian say, "I hope my dummy is okay."

I didn't laugh at Brian's joke until I saw Billy get up on wobbly legs and take a few steps. He was pale-white and a little disoriented, but other than a few scrapes and bruises on his arms and legs, he seemed fine. And so he lived to create havoc for another day!

Matthew 25:15 (NASB)... "To one he gave five talents, to another, two, and to another, one, each according to his own ability; and he went on his journey."

We attended Public School 138 or, as New Yorkers would say, "P.S. 138." This may seem like a rather odd name for a school, especially if you come from a place where schools are named after dead presidents or community leaders. In New York and the five boroughs, schools are still named "P.S. something-or-other," just as they were when I was growing up.

We (Tommy, Billy, Dorothy and I) would walk to school every morning. Leaving our towering environment and heading to school would be equivalent to leaving a king's palace and journeying into a forest of unknown. The neighborhood three-block journey to school consisted of all private homes with backyards, stoops, lots, fruit trees, and fenced-in dogs. We would be on our own, getting ready for school most of the time, so Tommy and Dorothy were responsible for my preparation for school and for getting me there in one piece.

By the time we made it to school, we were usually dirty from a random stop to climb a tree or to play with a stray dog. Catching snakes was one of our favorite activities while we headed to school in the mornings, lifting rocks and boards to try and find a snake camping underneath.

One morning, Billy caught a garden snake that we would normally let go into someone's garden before we arrived at school. This particular day, Billy decided not to set the snake free. Instead, he found a small brown bag and placed the snake inside of it, intending to bring it to school. One of the shortcut entrances into our school was through the cafeteria, and as we were passing through, Billy glanced into the kitchen and saw a large metal basin with tomato sauce inside of it. All of us knew what he was intending to do, and we ran as fast as we could to get out of the cafeteria. Sure enough, Billy opened the brown bag and after looking around to make sure the coast was clear, he lifted the snake from the bag and tossed it right into the large basin of tomato sauce. The lunch du jour was meatloaf, and to say the least, the Murray kids went home hungry that day.

Exodus 35:1 (NIV)… "Moses assembled the whole Israelite community and said to them, 'These are the things the LORD has commanded you to do.' "

We attended a school assembly every Friday. The school rule was that boys had to wear a white shirt and tie. If you came to school without your tie, a teacher would make you wear a cutout paper tie. If you came without a white shirt, you were not allowed to go to the assembly.

I always seemed to need the paper tie. That, combined with not having a white shirt at least once a month, made for more than a little friction with my teachers. Friday mornings in our house were more like a search-and-rescue operation. Our family did our wash on Saturdays, and by the time the following Friday rolled around, we would normally be digging through the hamper in search of clothes. By then, they were dirty and smelly, so with any luck, I might have a white shirt for assembly.

Dorothy and Tommy had the chore of doing the laundry. They would load a full shopping cart plus three extra pillowcases full of clothes. The clothes needed to be separated into two piles, one color and one white. If you overslept Saturday morning and missed wash day, you were out of luck and wore dirty clothes that week. The trip to the Laundromat was across Castle Hill Avenue and behind the stores. The whole operation took about two hours, and Dad would watch the clock for our return.

When Billy and I became of age, the job was handed down to us. Our Saturday mornings of fun and adventure now turned into child labor. The first day we walked into the Laundromat, we had the same thought. "How can we speed up this process?" The first thing we figured was that we could save time by not separating the colors from the whites. We found three empty machines and stuffed the clothes into them. As the machines were rolling, we added soap powder into each machine until the entire box was empty.

With time to kill, we walked to the luncheonette. As we walked in the owner, Willie, spotted us and immediately kicked us out because of previous offenses. So we decided to walk over to the department store only a few feet away because it had a small sit-down food counter to hang out at.

The counter had balloons hanging overhead for the purpose of selling ice cream sundaes at discounted prices. If you popped the correct balloon, you could win and pay only one penny. The odds were that you would pay the normal price.

Today Billy and I were feeling lucky. After popping one of the balloons, we took out the small piece of paper revealing the price. Immediately, we took off running because the price was the regular rate, and we couldn't afford it. We bolted out the door as the lady behind the counter began yelling and swearing that we would not be allowed back into the store.

Heading back to the Laundromat, hoping the wash was done, our wish came true as all three machines had stopped. Our luck ran out when we saw all the dryers were being used. It took two dryers to hold all our clothes. As Billy and I sat there waiting, one machine became available, so we thought it would be faster to just stuff the one machine with all of the clothes. Of course, before the clothes went into the machine, Billy insisted on first getting inside and going for a ride.

Accommodating his demands, he jumped into the dryer. As the machine started to spin, Billy was now tossing and tumbling inside the dryer, laughing and making faces through the glass window. The dryer was now heating up, so Billy's ride was over—but not before I leaned up against the door, refusing to let him out.

His laughing now turned into panic, screaming and crying for me to open the door. After a few minutes of hysteria with his kicking the dryer door, did I finally let him out. With only a few burn marks on his elbows, we stuffed the dryer and headed back up to the front of the stores.

As Billy and I were peeking into the luncheonette, one of the older guys named Aldo asked if we wanted to get even with Willie for kicking us out earlier. At the same time, we both shouted a big "YES!"

The layout in the luncheonette as you walked in the door was three phone booths to the left and the cash register to the right. Further in the store was a long food counter toward the back. Aldo handed us a dime along with a small piece of paper with a phone number on it and said, "When Willie goes to the back of the store, sneak in and get inside of the phone booth."

We clearly understood our instructions and as Willie was preoccupied with customers, we bolted into the phone booth. We dialed the number given to us, and that number happened to be for Willie's use only. The store phone was near the food counter, and as the phone rang, we could see Willie walking toward the back. Just as he was about to pick up the phone, we hung up on him. As our dime came back, we slipped the coin back into the slot, repeating the process about five times while watching Willie walk back and forth. Each time we hung up on him as he was about to answer.

By now, Billy and I were almost peeing on ourselves with laughter as we could hear Aldo and the other guys hooting and hollering with laughter outside. On our sixth try, Willie looked up from his register and spotted us.

With fright running down my spine, he gave me a cold hard stare. "We were busted!"

Willie came running from behind the register with a broomstick as Billy and I bolted from the phone booth. Running to the entrance, I realized I had left the dime in the return coin slot. I turned around and headed back to the booth, grabbing the dime and making it halfway out the door with the broomstick slicing down the back of my legs. Willie chased us halfway down the block as Aldo and the other guys taunted him with insults and profanities about his actions.

Making our way back to the Laundromat, we noticed the clothes had not stopped tumbling inside the dryer, so we decided to make our way back to the front of the stores. We walked back and forth from the Laundromat to the stores, and now five hours had passed since we started our wash.

We decided to sit there and wait for the dryer to stop spinning. Right then, our sister, Dorothy, walked in with a concerned look on her face and warning us about how angry Dad was. The three of us waited, watching the dryer tumble over and over and then immediately come to a halt.

Billy blurted out "Finally" as we walked toward the machine. When Billy reached for the door handle, he was shoved away by a tall woman screaming, "Get away from my clothes!"

We then realized our wash had been done for quite a while, and we found our clothes in the back of the Laundromat on a table where they were cold and all wrinkled. As Dorothy was gathering the clothes to put back in the basket, she yelled in horror as she held up what was once a white shirt that was now pink. "What did you guys do?"

Because of our genius idea of putting all of the clothes together, all the whites were now pinks. Dad did not give us the belt buckle, but it was embarrassing wearing pink shirts to school for the next couple of days. Without realizing it, we were now no longer put in charge of doing wash, upsetting both Tommy and Dorothy.

Job 37:10 (NIV) ... "The breath of God produces ice, and the broad waters become frozen."

One afternoon, Tommy and I walked home from school for lunch. After we had lunch, I dug around in the freezer, looking for something to snack on like a frozen ice pop. I happened to notice the top of the freezer was covered with ice.

In those days, the refrigerator-freezer was all you had, which was a lot compared to the ice boxes our parents had when they were growing up. The freezer inside of the refrigerator was a metal square about the size of a breadbox, and it always had a coating of icy condensation on the top of the unit.

The day was hot, and we had no ice pops, so I thought I would lick the ice on the top of the freezer to cool off. When I did, my tongue seemed to get stuck—though I couldn't imagine why! I panicked and quickly pulled off my tongue, ripping the skin on the surface of the tongue, taste buds and all. I screamed and started to cry piteously.

"What happened?" Tommy asked.

I tried to explain it to him, though it was difficult to talk at the time. When he didn't believe me, I retorted, "Try it yourself!"

Cynically, he walked to the refrigerator, opened the door, peered inside for a minute, leaned forward, and placed his tongue on top of the freezer unit. Strangely enough, his tongue got stuck—just like mine!

There was Tommy with his head in the refrigerator, his tongue stuck to the freezer, gurgling for help.

2 Samuel 23:2 (NIV) ... "The Spirit of the LORD *spoke through me; his word was on my tongue."*

I didn't know what to do except start to giggle. I knew from experience how much it would hurt to pull his tongue off the ice, but I thought it would be worse if he left it there any longer. "Pull as hard as you can," I suggested.

Tommy stayed stuck to the icebox for two to three minutes while trying to gain the courage to pull his tongue off. He finally pulled backward full force and fell back to the floor. His tongue was raw and bleeding worse than mine had.

All the way back to school, he complained about his tongue. "I should have believed you," he declared. Never before or after that day did my brother ever say he should have listened to my advice, but it sure felt good to hear it at least once!

Genesis 30:37 (NIV) ... "Jacob, however, took fresh-cut branches from poplar, almond and plane trees and made white stripes on them by peeling the bark and exposing the white inner wood of the branches."

Dragging ourselves to school one morning, Billy and I took a different route through an area that was called "the volcano." Smoke continually belched from the ground at the volcano, a dump with fires burning underground. This area was a dumping ground for everything from dirt to household goods and everything in between.

Billy was recalling a few weeks earlier when Gumby, he and I saved Blackie's life. Whenever we would rumble through the piles of tossed-out belongings of others, Blackie would always show up. Blackie was a fun-loving friendly dog whose owner allowed him to run wild, and everyone knew Blackie.

Gumby said he heard a faint growling sound coming from a sewer that was on the corner leaving the volcano. As we came closer, the distinct sound became louder. We could see that the sewer cap had been removed, and obviously, a dog was at the bottom of the sewer. Gumby was elected to go down into the sewer to see what the situation was.

Climbing down and squealing about the smell, he reached the bottom, and sure enough, he yelled back up, "It's Blackie!"

Blackie was rolled up in a rug someone had placed over the sewer after removing the cap. Blackie had inadvertently walked onto the rug, and like a trapped lion caught in a net, he fell to the bottom of the sewer. Gumby added, "Blackie's okay. The rug kept him from getting hurt."

"I'll go knock on his owner's door and let him know about Blackie being at the bottom of the sewer," Billy offered.

The fire department was called, and the rescuers were able to bring Blackie to the surface. The owner gave us a five-dollar reward for our efforts that we fought over all the way home—after we figured out that five did not divide evenly among three.

As Billy and I continued our walk to school, looking through piles of discarded junk, we found all kinds of office supplies. The jackpot was about ten boxes of "Bic" pens, which each box containing a dozen. We had enough pens to last us through the school year.

These Bic pens sported a hard metal clip connected to them so you could hook them to your top pocket.

That day while I was daydreaming (which was a normal pastime for me in school), I snapped the metal clip off of my pen and started to dig it into the top of my solid-wood desk. I liked occupying my mind this way to pass the time, so for more than a week I dug the clip of my pen into the top of the desk while the teacher droned on. With my dedicated effort, the desk now looked like a stripped tree with no bark. Still, the desk was also clean—something rare after all the use the desks got year after year.

I had given each kid a Bic pen from my jackpot, and like a wildfire, all the kids started frantically "shaving" their desks to look like mine. One boy was so excited about the prospect that the next day he brought a hunting knife to school to scrape his desk! Of course, he progressed faster because his scraping tool had a handle.

I don't know why our teacher didn't notice all of this frantic activity, but she didn't. One day when the principal came to talk to the class, he did notice the condition of the desks. I sat up straight with folded hands, thinking a reward was coming my way for how nice all our desks looked. Boy, was I in for a surprise when he became angry.

The entire class was disciplined, and of course, everyone was upset at me for starting the ball rolling. For the next week, I had to put up with spitballs, rubber bands, rolled-up paper, pens, and pencils thrown at the back of my head because of the principal's disciplinary action.

Joel 2:1 (NIV) … "Blow the trumpet in Zion; sound the alarm on my holy hill. Let all who live in the land tremble, for the day of the LORD is coming. It is close at hand—"

Chuck and Luis were two guys in school who would sometimes walk home with me at the end of the day. We would leave by way of the lunchroom entrance, and walk down a small hallway where the bright-red firebox was hung. We passed the firebox every day, but one day in particular, that box caught our attention. I felt as if it called our names. As we stood staring at the firebox, all of us were thinking the same thing at the same time: which one of us would pull the handle to set off the alarm. In a mere instant, Chuck finally pulled the handle, and alarms started going off throughout the school, both inside and outside.

We three ran as fast as we could, and we didn't stop until we made it back to the projects. Having gotten away with the prank once, we could not be stopped. For the next week, we set off the alarms every day after school. The following week, we decided we should probably stop before we got caught but, for some strange reason, on that Friday, we couldn't resist the temptation. As our treat before the weekend, we decided to pull the alarm handle one last time.

This was the day I got to set off the alarm. It was my first time, and I was scared to death. I grabbed the handle, squeezed my eyes shut, held my breath and pulled down. Sure enough, the sirens and alarms started to blast. My heart was pounding, but I felt exhilarated as I took off behind Chuck and Luis. "This is pretty exciting!" I thought...until out of the corner of my eye, I saw a door fly open, and someone was now chasing me.

I ran as fast as I could, gasping for air, and feeling a stitch starting to form in my side. When I glanced around, the person was still running and catching up to me rather quickly.

Before I could catch my breath, I was grabbed from behind and thrown to the ground. I tumbled for a few feet and abruptly came to a stop, flat on my back looking straight up into the beet-red face of an angry school custodian. I shook and grieved, as he passionately recounted the trouble I was in and the punishment I would endure. Forcefully, he marched me back to the school.

Sitting in the principal's office, and listening as he called my father, all I could think about was the beating I was going to get. I quickly concocted a story to tell him. "Chuck said if I didn't pull the alarm, he was going to beat me up."

When he was asked, Chuck of course denied the threat, and both of us had to stay after school for a week, writing "I will never pull the alarm box again" on the blackboard, over and over, until our hands were coated in chalk, and our wrists were sore. By the end of the week, I thought my hand would fall off.

Of course, Luis had a good laugh at both of us because the custodian never saw him. I did get disciplined by Dad, but worse than that was the fact that he would remind me of the incident for the rest of his life. In my father's eyes, this was one of the top ten stupidest things Johnny ever did in his life, and he never failed to remind me of it constantly.

"HIDEOUS" ONE-EYE JOHNNY

▲ ▲ ▲

PSALM 17:8 (NIV)… "KEEP me as the apple of your eye; hide me in the shadow of your wings."

As the school years passed, my dad became more bewildered over my poor school performance. When he would ask why I was doing poorly, I would always make up the lie that I couldn't see the blackboard. Dad finally decided to have my eyes checked by an optometrist, and at this point, I knew it was just a matter of time before he found out I was lying.

He had to take time off from work to take me to the eye doctor, and he wasn't happy about that, so we weren't off to a good start on the day of the examination. We got to Jacobi Hospital, and he couldn't find a parking spot. After about 45 minutes of driving around, we finally found a spot about five blocks away.

I just kept quiet during the walk to the hospital. I knew Dad wasn't happy! We took the elevator to the fifth floor, and when we got off, we saw that the waiting room was packed with people. We waited three hours to get into the clinic!

By this time, Dad was really upset over the waiting time. He tried to be patient when he was talking to the nurses, but I knew he wasn't in a good mood. As I sat there waiting, all I could think about was what excuse I would use to explain my school performance after Dad found out my eyes were fine.

We finally got out of the hallway and went into the clinic only to find that the clinic was clogged with people as well. We sat in the clinic for about an hour while my eyes were dilating, and then we were taken into a dark room where a doctor made me put my chin onto a cold metal bar and shined a bright light into my eyes. The doctor's breath was awful, and he kept stretching my eye open until I thought my eyelids would fall off.

Finally, he walked out mumbling something to himself. After a few minutes, he returned with another doctor who also looked at my right eye, and then they both walked out of the room, mumbling together.

Mark 5:26 (NIV) ... "She had suffered a great deal under the care of many doctors and had spent all she had, yet instead of getting better she grew worse."

Before long, the room was crowded with doctors, all poking my right eye and stretching the lid in every direction. I had no idea what was going on, but they explained their findings to my dad.

On the ride home, Dad was quiet, and I could tell he was worried about something. Finally, he said, "You are blind in one eye, and you need to have an operation. The back of your eye was torn open somehow, and the doctors said they need to take out your eye and sew it back together."

I remembered that the doctors had asked me if I'd ever banged my eye or poked it with anything. Of course, I told them about the arrow Tommy shot into my eye and about the time I fell onto the bulldozer stick shift.

Dad said the doctors told him that one or both of these injuries had probably done the damage to my eye. We went back to visit the doctors once a week until the day of the operation.

Dad was very concerned about my eye, and I noticed a change in the way he treated me after that first visit to the doctor. He gave me a lot of attention, and I thought he probably felt somehow guilty about the injury. My brother, Tommy, also felt guilty because his was the arrow that had caused some of the damage.

I don't know if I completely understood the seriousness of this injury or the surgery, but the great thing about it was that Dad made a rule that none of my older brothers could hit me or push me around because it could further damage my eye. Dad was even afraid to hit me if I did something wrong.

Luke 4:18 (NIV) … "The Spirit of the Lord is on me, because he has anointed me to proclaim good news to the poor. He has sent me to proclaim freedom for the prisoners and recovery of sight for the blind, to set the oppressed free."

I started to enjoy the "one-eye" situation because of the attention I was receiving. And, of course, even though my brothers were forbidden to do me physical harm, they did come up with a way to torment me. My new name was now "One-Eye Johnny."

Operation day came, and I was suddenly struck with an acute case of the heebie-jeebies. In my mind's view, the doctors were about to yank my eye out of its socket, lay it on a table with my eyeball connected by long stringy ligaments stretching to the inside of my eye socket, then with a sharp object, they would operate on it, slicing it like a knife through butter.

Once in the operating room, and at the doctor's request, I counted backward from ten—a simple task even for a kid who wasn't doing so well in school. I believed I would get to "one," and I would be asked to count backward again because I was so good at it. But I only got to nine and a half, and I was out cold!

I woke up in the recovery room and saw both Mom and Dad standing over me. I was surprised to see Mom because she was in and out of the hospital due to her drinking problem. Her presence told me exactly how serious my operation had been.

Again, the attention I was receiving from everyone was unprecedented in my young life, and I loved it. Of course, with the full knowledge I would use it to my advantage any chance I was able!

Isaiah 6:2 (NASB) ... "Seraphim stood above Him, each having six wings: with two he covered his face, and with two he covered his feet, and with two he flew."

Meanwhile, at night my entire bed was domed with clear plastic to keep out any germs. When it was time for me to go to sleep and everyone had left my room, I would panic, tearing at and ripping off the plastic cover. When the nurse came back to check on me, she scolded me. Still, I refused to let them put the plastic cover over the bed. They would put it up, and I would tear it down as soon as they left the room.

I was so annoying to them that during the day the nurses had picked out a game I could play and would describe my personality at the same time. The game was called "Trouble."

When I left the hospital, I had a large patch covering my right eye, and my face was swollen on that side. I only knew this because, before leaving the hospital, I secretly went (after being told not to) into the bathroom and pulled off the patch and gazed into the mirror to see what I looked like. I was a hideous one-eyed monster—at least I convinced myself of that assessment by the time I got home.

Acts 22:6 (NIV) … "About noon as I came near Damascus, suddenly a bright light from heaven flashed around."

A very heavy snow had fallen the night before I left the hospital, and when I walked out the door, the sun's reflection on the snow was so bright, it nearly blinded my only good eye. The air smelled fresh and clean, and I was happy to be outside—away from the smells of alcohol and ether.

The gang ran towards our car to greet me as we pulled up to the curb on Seward Avenue. The hill on the side of our building was the one every kid used for sledding after a heavy snow. The grass was mobbed with kids riding sleds, building snowmen, and enjoying nonstop snowball fights. The end of the sled path from the top of the hill was right outside our apartment window, and kids from other buildings came to ride on our hill. It was good to be home.

I was being prompted by Gumby to take the sled he was holding and take a ride down the hill. I looked at Dad for the okay, and he nodded his head with a yes, but added, "Be careful of your eye."

As I was on the top of the hill down on my knees ready to push off down the hill, my brother, Billy, asked if he could ride on top of me on the way down. His request was not some new idea that he had come up with. Kids were always catching a ride downhill on someone's back, but what occurred next, I believe, was a record setter in our neighborhood sledding adventures.

Genesis 11:4 (NIV) … "Then they said, 'Come, let us build ourselves a city, with a tower that reaches to the heavens, so that we may make a name for ourselves; otherwise we will be scattered over the face of the whole earth.' "

After Billy hopped on my back and we pushed off, Gumby screaming with laughter ran and jumped on top of Billy. Tommy T. with his Tarzan scream jumped on top of Gumby. Brian, hollering a pile-on scream, jumped on top of Tommy. Then Robbie joined in and jumped on top of Brian. There we were—a stack of six pancakes with me on the bottom of the pile being squeezed to death while everyone was laughing and hollering in sequence.

As the balancing act continued picking up more speed, we traveled down the hill, and with all the pressure on top of me, I couldn't steer the sled any longer; my only concern was being able to breathe. Kids were screaming as they jumped out of our path. We were headed straight ahead like a runaway freight train into a snow bank at the bottom of the hill. BAM! As we slammed into the snow bank, bodies went flying everywhere with screams of wild laughter, and the groaning was louder than before.

As everyone was getting up covered in snow from head to toe, Gumby looked at me and let out a loud screeching sound "YIKES!" The patch which covered my eye flew off after crashing into the snow bank, and I was now exposed for the hideous one-eyed monster I had pictured myself to be back in the hospital bathroom mirror.

I took off running with an apprehensive trail of onlookers, following right behind me into my apartment. Dad patched me back up in no time, and I was as good as new.

Matthew 6:28 (NASB) … "And why are you worried about clothing? Observe how the lilies of the field grow; they do not toil nor do they spin."

Getting ready to conquer the snow was an adventure in our house. Our hall closet held about twenty single black snow boots all identical looking, just different sizes. You had to sit on the floor and go through the boots for about fifteen minutes to find two of the same size. Finding hats and matching gloves required the same drill. I would dig through big brown boxes filled to the brim with hats and gloves of all sizes, finally finding a hat to fit my head, and hopefully two matching gloves that fit my growing hands. This stash of winter wear was what Dad brought home from work, the result of his rummaging through other people's trash.

I couldn't wait to get out into the snow. I grabbed another item rescued from the sanitation department—a sled and ran down the hall to go outside to meet the gang. As I came out of the building, Billy said, "The gang's going up to Castle Hill Avenue to ride the buses. Put the sled away!"

I just ran to our kitchen window, knocked and handed the sled to Jimmy. After dropping the sled smack down in the middle of the kitchen floor, Jimmy jumped out the window to join us only to whine and cry walking back into the building after being told he needed to stay home.

Colossians 2:19 (NIV) ... "They have lost connection with the head, from whom the whole body, supported and held together by its ligaments and sinews, grows as God causes it to grow."

The snow was deep that day, and, as we came to Castle Hill Avenue, the traffic was moving cautiously. Matthew, a friend of Brian, Gumby and Tommy T., was also with us, and they all went to Saint John Vianney, the Catholic school across the street from our building.

Gumby, Tommy T, Billy, Brian, Matthew and I lined up at the bus stop, waiting for the bus to arrive. When I said, "I don't have a bus pass," they started to laugh. Matthew then explained, "We aren't riding *in* the bus; we're riding *behind* it in the snow."

We could hear the bus arrive as the tires were wrapped in chains, which made loud clanging and crunching sounds in the deep snow as it approached the curb. The driver stopped the bus, and the passengers got on. Then he took off slowly, with Matthew, Billy, Gumby, Brian and Tommy T. running behind, trying to grab the bumper of the bus. Once they did, they slid on their boots as the bus pulled them in the snow.

I ran too, but I couldn't find a spot to hold on because too many guys were already holding on. As I watched them sliding down Castle Hill Avenue behind the bus, the snow started coming down harder. The bus picked up speed, and most of the guys lost their footing. They were now being dragged in the snow by the bus while holding on to the bumper for dear life. One by one, they lost their grip and fell off, tumbling into the snow and laughing. Matthew and Billy held on the longest, going about twenty blocks to the train station on Westchester Avenue.

James 1:12 (ESV) … "Blessed is the man who remains steadfast under trial, for when he has stood the test he will receive the crown of life, which God has promised to those who love him."

I stood with anticipation, waiting with the others for the next bus. This time I was determined to get a spot in the line. I was scared, but I had to do this or be labeled a chicken. As the youngest in the group, I was always the brunt of their jokes, and I didn't like it very much!

The next bus approached, and we waited for our chance. As it pulled away, we ran to grab a spot on the back. There was a lot of yelling and laughing as I got my grip. Gumby was yelling at me to hold on and not to let go. I made it all the way to the next bus stop without falling off. Gumby and I made it halfway to the train station, watching the others fall away behind us.

I turned my head away from the bus tires, squinting to keep the flying snow out of my eyes. At that moment, Billy and Matthew passed us hanging onto another bus and heading back to the projects in the opposite direction. Gumby yelled at me to jump off. He said, "Hurry up and we can catch up to Billy and Matthew. Their bus is about to make a stop."

We jumped off, ran across Castle Hill Avenue, and made it just in time to join Billy and Matthew on the back of their bus headed down to the projects. It was dark now, and it had gotten cold. The snow was blowing into our faces and stinging our cheeks. I could hardly hold onto the bus because my gloves had gotten wet and slippery, and my fingers were frozen and stiff. Somehow, I summoned the strength to make it back to the projects.

We let go of the bus in between bus stops, tumbling head over heels and laughing as we were falling on top of each other. When we got up, we looked like badly made snowmen. We walked up to the stores where Tommy T. and Brian were waiting for us in the luncheonette.

Job 9:30 (KJV) … "If I wash myself with snow water, and make my hands never so clean."

Willy and Charlotte were the owners of the luncheonette. They would usually let us hang around inside for a while; but when the 9:00 p.m. *Daily News* delivery truck came, we had to go outside because too many people were waiting in the store to buy the paper. Someone from my family would, of course, be among the crowd, waiting to get Dad the *Daily News Night Owl*.

My sister, Dorothy, was there on this particular night, and I had to convince her not to tell Dad she had seen me. As the newspaper truck pulled up to the luncheonette, we decided to hop on the back and go for a ride when the truck was about to leave. The news truck had a small ledge on the back where you could sit down. As the truck took off, Matthew, Tommy T., Billy and I grabbed the ledge and jumped on by holding onto the back door handle. Gumby held on as he slid along behind in the snow. Gumby fell off when the driver increased his speed, but we weren't able to jump off because the truck was going too fast.

The driver made every green light for a few blocks and then decided to run the red lights he encountered. He took the small side streets past the sanitation department, then over the Union Port Bridge, past the drive-in movie theater and ended up over near the Whitestone Bridge—quite a few miles away from the projects. All the while, we sat on the back of the truck, holding on tightly and waiting for a chance to get our feet back on the ground.

At last he stopped the truck. We jumped down into the snow and ran off to the safety of a sidewalk. It was pitch-black, and the snow was blowing in circles as the wind buffeted us from all sides. We were freezing! Our curfew was 9:00 p.m., and Billy and I wondered out loud about going home to face Dad. "Maybe we should just run away or stay out all night." We tried to convince the other guys to run away with us, but it was too cold, and everyone was hungry. A beating from Dad seemed a small price to pay for a warm blanket, dry clothes and some food.

James 1:5 (NIV) … "If any of you lacks wisdom, you should ask God, who gives generously to all without finding fault, and it will be given to you."

Billy and I decided to take a chance and go home. When we got to our building, we figured it was better to sneak in through our bedroom window. But as we climbed through the window, Dad was sitting there waiting with belt buckle in his hand.

I looked at Billy and said, "Me first" because I just wanted to get to bed. As Dad was about to rip into me, all I said was, "Billy made me stay out late."

Dad turned to him with the buckle, and it was all over! After taking his beating and mine, Billy was so angry that he wouldn't let me sleep with him, so I had to sleep on the couch. Still I'd had my first "bus-slide" adventure, and now I was warm and dry. And I had narrowly escaped another encounter with the dreaded belt buckle, so a night on the couch was fine with me!

"GET YOUR NEWS HERE"

▲ ▲ ▲

MARK 1:15 (NIV) … " 'THE time has come,' he said. 'The kingdom of God has come near. Repent and believe the good news!' "

When we woke up in our apartment in the middle of winter, it was freezing cold. Before the heat "came up," we would turn on the oven and sit as close to the open door as we dared. The cold was annoying, but there was a happy feeling when the heat from the oven penetrated my body. The one thing more annoying was having to listen to the "Pledge of Allegiance" drifting out over the crisp, winter morning air, courtesy of the students of St. John Vianney Catholic school.

In our school, we said the "Pledge of Allegiance," but the kids in St. John's had to sing it. Every morning, the nuns would ring the bells and, before the children were allowed to enter the school, they would sing. The song was beautiful, but it wore thin after years of hearing it on every morning of every school day.

At that time, my brother Billy and I had a paper route. We would wake up around 6:00 a.m. to deliver the papers. The route started two blocks from our building, and it was seven blocks long, all private houses. We would run as fast as we could up and down the stairs of each house, so we could finish quickly. In the winter, we would slip and slide down the street in the packed snow and ice, pulling our wagon filled with newspapers.

One house had about ten stairs with the mailbox slot on the door. During the winter, we would slide the paper through the slot. Billy had just inserted the paper on the top step and turned to me laughing that he hit the cat inside the house right on the head. I saw it coming but had no time to react.

All the steps were ice, and the next step Billy took sent him sliding, bumping and slamming his body all the way down the stairs. He rolled off the sidewalk and into the street.

He was hurt bad, and he could not get up. The street was deserted except for the two of us, and I began to realize I was on my own. I was pleading with him to get up, and he was just moaning and grumbling.

"I need to go home," he moaned. I would have to finish the paper route alone. As I watched him hobble down the block, I was just hoping he would be okay. As I continued the paper route, it now took me longer doing it alone, and the freezing weather was starting to take a toll on me. I could not stop thinking of the flop I had seen Billy take all the way down those stairs.

As I walked into the house half-frozen, I looked up to see Billy standing there with a big fat grin on his face, indicating he was fine. He had just pulled a fast one on me. He wasn't hurt at all from the tumble at the top of the stairs, but he decided to fake injury to make me finish the route alone.

I was so angry, and as I was about to start screaming at him, I started to laugh and couldn't stop. All I could see in my mind was Billy's tumbling down the stairs. Hurt or not, the sight of his coming down the stair made me laugh for a long time.

Matthew 6:11 (NIV) … "Give us today our daily bread."

The last stop after our paper route was St. John Vianney. Every morning, a delivery man dropped off big, soft pretzels for the school to sell during lunch time. He left the pretzels at the front door in a covered basket at about 7:00 a.m., and, on most mornings, Billy and I would help ourselves to a pretzel breakfast. On Saturdays and Sundays, we didn't need to rush home to get to school on time, so we would walk over to the Big Apple supermarket. There, we would help ourselves to the racks of pies and cakes that another dedicated delivery man left out in front of the store.

One morning, I had a brilliant idea to get back at Billy for the stunt he had pulled with falling down the stairs and faking an injury. I pulled a cherry pie from the pie rack as Billy turned toward me, and I smashed him right in the face with it. I couldn't stop laughing before he pulled a pie from the rack and smashed it into my face.

Together we came up with the idea of wheeling the entire rack of pies home for a pie fight with our buddies later that day. Before a pie fight emerged, every pie was eaten by friends and family before noon. The pie rack was converted into a rolling clubhouse. We took the rack into the little lot near St. John's, and after a few hours using a bunch of plywood and extra wheels from another shopping cart, we had ourselves a six-foot clubhouse on wheels.

Heading opposite of Castle Hill Avenue on Seward Avenue was a steep hill and at the bottom Olmstead Avenue crossed Seward. Tommy T., Gumby, Billy, Jerry and I pushed our clubhouse on wheels across Seward Avenue. All of us were thinking the same thought as we looked down toward the bottom of Seward Avenue.

Minutes later, everyone was hanging onto the clubhouse screaming as we went speeding down Seward Avenue. The crossroad,

Olmstead Avenue, was getting closer and closer, and our only means of steering was leaning from one side to the other. I jumped off the runaway clubhouse along with Jerry and Gumby. The three of us tumbled down Seward Avenue with our bodies sliding on the pavement, scraping off the skin on our elbows and knees.

Meanwhile, Billy and Tommy T. were both on the roof of the runaway clubhouse leaning this way and that in order to steer while heading straight into the intersection of Seward Avenue and Olmstead. Jerry, Gumby and I were now up and running behind the clubhouse, somehow hoping to get the clubhouse under control because of the cars whizzing through the intersection. Both Billy and Tommy T. were leaning as far as possible to the left for a turn at the bottom of the hill. As they were coming into the left hand turn, we could see the clubhouse start to tip over completely to the left with Billy and Tommy T. screaming at the top of their lungs.

Every car going through the intersection came to a screeching halt as the clubhouse started its descent sideways to the ground. Watching Billy and Tommy T. on the roof, we saw Tommy T. grab hold of Billy, who was smaller than he was, and use him as a safety cushion as they flew through the air.

When Tommy T. and Billy landed on the concrete, Tommy T. was on top of Billy who screamed in agony with his body being crushed and bruised. When the ride was over, Billy had deep cuts and scrapes on his face, legs and arms as Tommy T. was laughing hysterically, bragging about his fast thinking action by using Billy as his "life preserver."

Tommy T. continued his laughter as we left the pile of rubble—formerly our clubhouse—in the middle of the street and headed back up Seward Avenue toward our building. Sitting in the hallway licking and massaging our bruises and scrapes, we had to listen to Tommy T. go on and on about being the only one without a scrape or bruise from our scuttled adventure.

Romans 16:17 (NIV) ... "I urge you, brothers and sisters, to watch out for those who cause divisions and put obstacles in your way that are contrary to the teaching you have learned. Keep away from them."

Tommy T. was the first one to get a paper route. His route consisted of his building (building 2140), my building (2160) and the route of private houses he gave to Billy and me. There was no unselfishness in his gift. Quite simply, he could never finish the entire route and still make it to school on time. When Tommy gave us the route, he, of course, kept the two buildings for himself. Tommy would laugh at the thought that after giving Billy and me the private houses, his route was now a piece of cake. When it rained, he would laugh even harder as he watched from his dry spot in our building, while we were soaking wet, walking into the building after we finished. Fridays were collection days, and we had to go to each house to collect the money for the papers we had delivered that week. We got the tips, and that amount usually came out to about $10, which Billy and I would split.

Exodus 28:14 (NIV) ... "and two braided chains of pure gold, like a rope, and attach the chains to the settings."

Tommy T. and Jerry always hung out together. When it came to imagination, these two bad boys had more imagination than Billy and Brian, if that were possible. Jerry had a certain wiggle about him when he walked, which is why we called him "Wiggles." Jerry, of course, hated the nickname. Jerry would chase anyone who called him "Wiggles," and if he caught the name caller, he would smack the offender around because he was a fairly tough guy.

One day, we were horsing around on the grass, and I dared to call Jerry by his nickname. He got angry and started to chase me, screaming all the while about what he would do to me when he caught me. I just kept laughing because I knew he couldn't catch me. He yelled at me some more, telling me he hated that nickname, and I yelled back to ask why. "You look like a bowl of 'Jello!' " I yelled. "I think the name fits just fine."

My taunting him had the effect of swatting at an angry bee, and Jerry began to run faster, chasing me in circles. A metal chain-link rope separated the grass from the sidewalk, and I kept jumping over the chain ropes to stay out of Jerry's reach. Back and forth, over the ropes and back again, I jumped and Jerry would follow.

Jerry was mere inches from catching me when I grabbed one of the chain ropes, and shook it in a circle. At that moment, Jerry took his next jump, and the rope did exactly what I thought it would do, tripping him! He landed face first, falling onto the cement sidewalk. After a moment of silence, I began to realize that Jerry was really hurt.

Lamentations 3:16 (NIV) ... "He has broken my teeth with gravel; he has trampled me in the dust."

He started to cry and tears streamed down his cheeks as he stood up with wobbling, weak knees. He had blood on his face, pants, and shirt. The sidewalk was even bloody.

As I looked closer, I realized that he had two front teeth missing, and blood was running freely from his nose. Scrapes and bruises decorated his face.

I was standing about ten feet away by now, just watching in horrified silence. I started blubbering an apology to Jerry, "Oh, man, I didn't want that to happen!" I cried, feeling the sting of tears and humiliation. "I'm sorry, Jerry."

Jerry was still crying, and as he wiped at the blood from his mouth and nose, he realized his front teeth were missing. "Oh, no!" he cried in horror. "Mom is going to be furious about this!

Job 9:25 (NASB) … "Now my days are swifter than a runner; They flee away, they see no good."

"Please help me find my teeth." He dropped to his knees, tears still flowing, and started brushing through the grass looking for his missing teeth. I felt obligated to help, and after a minute or so, I found what looked like some pieces of his teeth, blood-stained and shattered.

"Jerry, here are your teeth," I said sheepishly, holding up the bloody pieces.

Jerry surveyed the damage for a moment, and then screamed an obscenity at me through his bleeding lips. Just like that, he was on his feet and chasing me again. So I took off running again, heading around the back of the building. I ran as fast as I could into the building. I slammed opened the door to the staircase, then shot through another door to the main hallway, with Jerry right on my heels.

My apartment door was in sight as I ran down the hall as fast as possible. I got to the door, grabbed the doorknob and twisted it, praying the door was not locked.

Revelation 3:8 (NIV) … "I know your deeds. See, I have placed before you an open door that no one can shut. I know that you have little strength, yet you have kept my word and have not denied my name."

Still praying and twisting the doorknob, the door opened with Jerry just inches from my back. I pushed on the door and dove into the house, immediately slamming the door shut behind me.

I was out of breath from the chase, standing against the door, wheezing and puffing, while Jerry banged hard enough to wake the dead.

"You're paying for my teeth! I mean it! You're paying for my teeth," he repeated over and over like a broken record. I quietly leaned against the door, listening carefully to hear when he might walk away. At last, he left, dragging himself down the hall, still crying and moaning about his teeth. I relaxed and breathed a sigh of relief, knowing I was safe at least until we met again.

Matthew 11:28 (NIV) ... "Come to me, all you who are weary and burdened, and I will give you rest."

"Wow! That was sure a close one!" I thought. For the first time since I'd come into the apartment, I looked away from the door and realized that my father and Billy were watching me, with eyebrows raised and waiting for my explanation. I was in a panic, frantically trying to remember exactly what Jerry had said that my father might have heard.

Dad grabbed me by the collar of my jacket. "What in the world did you do now?" he sternly demanded.

"Nothing...Nothing," I blurted.

"Then why was your friend banging on the door?"

"Uh, we were playing a game."

But Dad wasn't buying my it. "Game? That was no game. You are up to no good. I know it." He slapped me hard in the back of the head and then threw me to the floor. I laid there wailing and protesting, "I didn't do anything. Honest, I didn't!"

1 John 2:21 (ESV) ... "...no lie is of the truth."

And just when I thought I had Dad convinced, he threw me a curve-ball. "Oh, yeah?" he shouted. "What else went on today? What's this I hear about you standing there watching Billy getting beat up by Robbie? I told you guys to stick together and protect each other!"

I should have kept my head down and my mouth shut, but instead I blurted, "Yeah, well, he deserved it! He was annoying Robbie for no reason." I was still crying and in a panic now because my offenses were piling up.

Dad looked really angry and said, "And you deserve this!" He started to unbuckle his belt.

I pleaded, assuring him that I would not do anything like that again. But all Dad could say was "You're absolutely right it won't happen again!" He soundly disciplined me with his belt across my back and legs.

Dad worked as a garbage man, and he lifted heavy garbage cans all day. He was strong, and his punishments always hurt. I took off running toward the back of the apartment, with Dad yelling for me to stay in my room and out of his sight for the rest of the night. As I gingerly assessed the damage to my back and legs, I thought about my friends. When they got in trouble, they either received a scolding or a beating. "Why is it, that, in our family, we kids always get both?" I wondered.

Exodus 20:15 (NASB) … "You shall not steal."

Billy and I had the paper route for about a month when, one Friday evening, as I was collecting money from our customers, a not-so-funny thing happened. You see, Billy and I would take turns collecting the money, and on this particular Friday, it was my turn to collect.

The first customer opened the door and said that Tommy T. had already collected the money. I was puzzled. I went to the next house and was told that Jerry had been there to collect the money. Sure enough, every customer said Jerry or Tommy T. had made the collection.

To say I was pretty upset was putting it mildly. I just envisioned both of them sitting in the luncheonette sloshing down a few milkshakes and having a good laugh on Billy and me! Running into the house, I told Billy what had happened.

Billy suggested that we go to Jerry's house and take back our money. Jerry wasn't home, but his Mom was there. After we explained the situation, she assured us that Jerry would pay back every penny, and that he would be disciplined appropriately. We smirked at each other, knowing Jerry's mom was in no joking mood now. Next, we had to go see our boss, Mr. B., who lived in building 635 and explain why we didn't have the collection money.

1 Kings 3:25 (NIV) … "He then gave an order: 'Cut the living child in two and give half to one and half to the other.'"

Mr. B. was in charge of all the paper routes in the area, including delivering the papers to us in the early morning. We told Mr. B. what Tommy T. had done, and he cleverly decided to fire him and split the two buildings on his route between Billy and me.

Billy got building 2140, and I got our building; building 2160. Billy was a little upset because he wanted our building, but he took what Mr. B. gave him with no complaints. My new route was great! It only took 20 to 30 minutes to run from the first door on the twelfth floor to the last door on the first floor, and I didn't have to worry about the weather because my entire route was now indoors. Even better was listening to the beating Jerry was getting from his mom. From the first floor in the grass, we could hear Jerry four stories up crying like a baby as his mom whipped him with a belt.

PICKING UP STRAYS

▲ ▲ ▲

Ezekiel 34:16 (ESV) … *"I will seek the lost, and I will bring back the strayed, and I will bind up the injured, and I will strengthen the weak, and the fat and the strong I will destroy. I will feed them in justice."*

Throughout the projects, kids always seemed to come home with stray dogs. We were no different. Every kid would take turns asking their parents to see if they could keep the dog. We hardly ever got to keep one in our house, but we did build clubhouses, and we always kept the dogs there.

There was the little lot next to St. John's, and that was where we built our "dog clubhouse." Sometimes we had as many as five or six dogs crammed into that little building. I would wake up in the morning to do my paper route, and I would find the renegade Brownie sleeping right at our door.

Brownie was my favorite. A great dog, he always followed me on my paper route. I was glad to have him at 6:00 a.m. because it was a little spooky walking down the stairs alone. I would hear a creak on the stairs or in the floor, and I'd run like a jackrabbit. Snowball was another good dog who would sometimes go with Brownie and me on the paper route.

I had no idea where the dogs came from, until one day Gumby, Eddie C., Tommy T. and Matthew let me come with them and let me in on the big secret.

Proverbs 24:11 (ESV) ... "Rescue those who are being taken away to death; hold back those who are stumbling to the slaughter."

We journeyed for about an hour, over highways past railroad tracks, under bridges, and past places I have never seen before. I trusted nervously that these guys knew where they were going. My thoughts drifted back to a few weeks earlier after the guys had made the same trip. Tommy T. had stormed into the lobby of our building huffing and puffing and looking white as a ghost. After regaining his composure and catching his breath, he went on to tell us that after they snatched up a few dogs from this secret location somewhere in the South Bronx, they were accosted at knifepoint by two older teenagers, threatening their lives.

Tommy T. said he took off running as soon as he saw the knives and that, as he looked back, he saw both Gumby and Matthew with the knives at their throats. We immediately gathered a few more guys together, along with a few choice weapons as we were now on a rescue mission. Our big bad rescue mission talk quickly evaporated as Gumby and Matthew came walking into the building.

The guys explained that after the thugs took their money and the dogs they had rescued, they were told to run as fast as they could and not to stop or look back. They started running and didn't stop for seven blocks, and they were grateful just to be alive.

Finally, we came to the secret location I had heard so much about. This large building had a sign with the letters "ASPCA" on it displayed above the door. I had no clue what the "ASPCA" was, but then Eddie explained it this was the place people brought dogs to be killed.

We stood outside waiting for someone to bring a dog to the door. When someone came to drop off a dog, we intended to ask them to give us the dog instead.

Luke 18:35 (NASB) ... "As Jesus was approaching Jericho, a blind man was sitting by the road begging."

Finally, after 30 minutes or so a man approached the building with his dog and started to open the door of the ASPCA to go inside. Tommy T. told him that the ASPCA would kill the dog if he left it there, but if he gave the dog to us, he could be assured that we would take care of it.

The man hesitated and then started to walk inside.

Tommy T. wasn't about to let this go without a fight. He fell to his knees and started to cry real tears, begging the man for the dog.

The man probably thought Tommy T. was crazy, but he gave him the dog anyway. This newest member to our gang was a beagle named Bootsy. Eddie C. kept Bootsy for about fifteen years, and she had about six litters of puppies, one as beautiful as the next. She was a great dog!

Lamentations 3:7 (CEV) ... "God built a fence around me that I cannot climb over, and he chained me down."

After that, I would go to the ASPCA often with the same group of guys. After all, we were on a mission to save these dogs. The staff inside the building did finally catch on to what we were doing, and they would chase us away whenever they saw us.

One day Gumby had a real brainstorm. Behind the ASPCA building was a fenced-in kennel that was accessible through a vacant lot. Dozens of dogs were held captive there. Gumby said we should come back after dark with a pair of fence clippers and rescue the dogs.

That is exactly what we did! One night after dark, we took the largest pair of fence clippers we could find—so large in fact that it took two guys to carry them—and we headed off to the ASPCA to rescue the ill-fated dogs.

I was scared to death the cops would catch us, and my heart was beating like a drum. It was dark and spooky behind the building, and I glanced from side-to-side, looking for any sign that we had been discovered.

Gumby and Matthew clipped away at the fence. All the dogs were now frantically barking louder and louder! We did our best to calm them down by calling out every dog name we knew, including Brownie, Lucky, Spot, Blackie, Duke, Lady, Lassie and on and on until most had calmed down while Gumby continued to work. Finally, he cut away enough of the fencing making it possible to squeeze through and climb down into the area where all the dogs were housed.

2 Corinthians 5:13 (NIV) … If we are "out of our mind," as some say, it is for God; if we are in our right mind, it is for you

Gumby jumped into the pit first. He sent up a howl about landing smack into a pile of dog waste. The dogs were excited, jumping on him as if they somehow knew he had come to their rescue. Eddie C. jumped down next, cautiously avoiding the dog crap.

Gumby and Eddie C. started to pass the dogs up to us, one by one. We retrieved about six dogs from the pit when someone hissed, "I think I see a cop car!"

We all went into a panic. We still had to get Eddie C. and Gumby out of the pit. We now had dogs running everywhere. Total chaos reigned! No one knew whether to hide, or bolt and run. "Which way should we go?" We couldn't very well leave Gumby and Eddie down there!

I was terrified. Then concern for our friends was overcome by our fear and panic, and we all took off running through the vacant lot and across a highway, with the dogs in hot pursuit. Suddenly, we heard a loud screeching noise and an immediate loud thump! One of the dogs we had freed had been hit by a car. We stopped in our tracks, unsure what to do next. We ran back to see if the dog was alive, but he wasn't moving.

The driver, along with others who had stopped to help, started to ask us all sorts of questions. Spurred on by our fear of being jailed, we ran off toward the projects, with the rest of the dogs following at our heels.

Somehow, Gumby and Eddie C. managed to crawl out of the pit, and our entire team of "criminals" found their way back to the projects unscathed.

Luke 12:18 (NIV) … "Then he said, 'This is what I'll do. I will tear down my barns and build bigger ones, and there I will store my surplus grain.'"

Back at the clubhouse, we caught our breath and counted heads. We had all the dogs stuffed into our tiny hideaway, and it was clear we didn't have room for one more animal, even if it was a chihuahua.

Once our hearts stopped racing and we realized that we had pulled off our dog rescue caper without getting caught, we became doubly brave. We decided we wanted to go back for more dogs, but we knew we couldn't even think about doing that until we built a bigger clubhouse.

As we discussed our plans for a new clubhouse, we heard movement and a shuffling sound outside the doorway of the clubhouse. It was pitch black outside, so we spooked ourselves into thinking it was the law finally catching up to us. As the shadowy figure passed the front door several times, we figured it wasn't the law but someone up to no good. Our plan was to all run out of the clubhouse at the same time and jump on whoever it was moving about.

On the count of three, moving swiftly and howling loudly, we jumped onto the suspecting stranger. As we piled on, we could hear a faint sound, then Gumby yelled, "It's Eddie V.!"

Our neighborhood had a few homeless wanderers, and Eddie V. was one of the friendlier and nicer ones who lived down near the mountains in a shanty. As Eddie V. pulled himself from the bottom of the pile, stood and brushed the dust and dirt off his body, he turned and held two quart bottles of Schaefer beer into the air screaming the word "Celarybrat."

Eddie V. was a Spanish guy in his late twenties or early thirties who was unable to speak English very well. Gumby knew Eddie better than any of us and also understood him better. Gumby said Eddie V. had been yelling profanities when we had tackled him to the ground, and the other word was "celebrate," meaning he wanted to share his beer with us.

The celebration was about to begin as Eddie V. and Matthew held the quarts of beer high in the air. We only had one little problem left and that was no one had a bottle opener for the beer bottles. Some of the suggestions made were to pull the cap along a rock, or to use a stick to pull the cap off. Eddie V. had a bewildered look on his face as he took the bottle away from Mathew, placed the bottle top in his mouth, and with his teeth, ripped the cap right off the bottle. We were all astonished! Then, he did the same with the second one. Loud cheers blasted from the gang as we passed the bottles around, all taking gulps of the beer as if we were drunken sailors just back from the high seas.

Psalm 91:1 (KJV) … "He that dwelleth in the secret place of the most High shall abide under the shadow of the Almighty."

Behind the stores on Castle Hill, past two more project buildings, we scouted some much larger lots and picked one to build our larger clubhouse. Building clubhouses was pretty simple for us because of all the construction going on in the area. We would simply help ourselves to plywood, nails, beams, and whatever other material was needed from the construction sites late at night.

We knew that our new clubhouse couldn't be seen from the street, and felt our secret would be safe in that location. We built the new and improved, expanded clubhouse and collected more dogs, until we had twelve animals living together under one roof. We were quite proud of our little rescue project!

One early morning, we were walking to the clubhouse from the projects, talking nonsense as usual. We were still some distance away when we saw dark black puffs of smoke coming from the vicinity of our new clubhouse.

1 Samuel 24:14 (NIV) … "Against whom has the king of Israel come out? Who are you pursuing? A dead dog? A flea?"

We ran as fast as we could, afraid of what we might see when we got there. As we came closer and the clubhouse was in full view, we saw a crew of firemen quenching the fire with their hoses. It was our clubhouse all right—totally destroyed! Every dog had died in the fire, burned to death, and their remains lay under the piles of soaked, burnt-smelling wood.

We stood a distance away from the fire, as instructed by the firemen, staring in disbelief, as they finished their work. Many of us cried in silence for the animals we had come to love. When they were finished, the firemen told us that the fire had been set on purpose with gasoline.

We were all visibly shaken as the police arrived and questioned us, asking if we knew who might have done this terrible thing. We had a good idea of who might be responsible, and we knew that one day that person would pay for what they had done. We never forgot this terrible incident, and although we never told the police who was responsible, eventually, we avenged the crime.

Our dog rescue mission ended after that day. We did have dogs after that, but it was never the same. The excitement and that wonderful feeling of having saved our fond friends for a higher purpose was gone. We lost our little buddy companions in the ashes of that terrible fire—the day that twelve dogs died at the hands of an arsonist.

BUILDING 2160 LOBBY CREW

▲ ▲ ▲

REVELATION 13:3 (NKJV) … "AND I saw one of his heads as if it had been mortally wounded, and his deadly wound was healed. And all the world marveled and followed the beast."

I lived right down the hall from the lobby of building 2160, where the gang would hang out. Our lobby had seventy mailboxes on each side, and right below the mailboxes was the vent for the heat where we would sit to stay warm during the winter.

I lived on one side of the lobby, and Brian lived on the other side. Most everyone else in our gang of friends lived in building 2160, with the exception of a few stragglers who lived in other project buildings and came to hang out in our building lobby. The front of our building had two doors with large plate-glass windows, one door on each side of the lobby. The rest of the lobby was also glass, so if you were standing in front of our building, you could look inside and see what was happening.

One day, Brian was amusing himself with the front door, hanging and doing chin ups on the metal bar that made the door swing open. The bar became bent by his weight, so now the door would only open about ten inches. Brian also made the wonderful discovery that, with his unintentional modification, the door would now snap back into the face of any unsuspecting person who tried to open it.

We would sit for hours at our observation point in front of the mailboxes, watching the people come in and out of the building, banging their heads on the door as it swung back into their faces. When it was a good, solid bang on the head, we'd laugh wildly. Sometimes, people would yell at us, telling us how evil we were, but others were too embarrassed to say anything. They would yell or yip, wince, rub their heads and keep going.

I think most of the people who came through those doors were afraid to say anything because there were always at least five to ten guys hanging out in the lobby, and most people were certainly not up for a useless argument. At the end of every day, the police would show up and kick us out of the lobby, telling us all to go home. The next day, we'd be back again.

1 John 4:1 (MSG) ... "My dear friends, don't believe everything you hear. Carefully weigh and examine what people tell you. Not everyone who talks about God comes from God. There are a lot of lying preachers loose in the world."

I was still quite gullible. I was starting to test and push my boundaries now, but I hadn't outgrown my absolute belief in what the older guys told me. Looking back now, I am reminded of a time, years before the Lobby Crew, when George C. told me that there was a money tree down in the lots near the second mountain. He said that he would walk down to the money tree every morning and pick coins and dollar bills from its branches—enough to last him for the day. "If you behave," he said, "I will show you the tree."

I followed him all day, nagging him to take me to the money tree. Then after hours of my nagging, he finally told me that he had made up the entire story.

I refused to believe him and continued to follow and nag him in front of all his friends to the point of embarrassment. Frustrated and angry, he ran home as I followed. He ran into the elevator ahead of me and zipped up to the twelfth floor. I caught the next elevator and bolted up to twelve, banging on his door and wanting the secret location of the money tree.

Mrs. C. opened the door and invited me in. George was in the back room, hiding and dreading the fact that he had ever said anything to me. Mrs. C. softened me up with a bunch of snacks until I forgot all about George. The picture of the money tree stayed in my head for years, until I finally realized that George really had been pulling my leg!

Matthew 10:16 (ESV)… "Behold, I am sending you out as sheep in the midst of wolves, so be wise as serpents and innocent as doves."

I was a little older now, but I still hadn't learned all there was to learn! It was a day like any other, with the group happily sitting in front of the heat vents below the mailboxes in the lobby. Brian suddenly jumped up and went running into his apartment, as if on a mission. The rest of us were curious but too lazy to follow him, so we stayed at our posts and waited for him to come back.

After a while, Brian returned, munching on an apple. We asked him where he had gotten the apple, and he told us he had an apple tree in his apartment. We all got a laugh out of that reply.

But I was still in my "gullible years." I believed him. An apple tree in your apartment seemed like a cool thing to have. Jerry stared at Brian as he ate his apple, commenting on how hungry he had gotten and telling Brian that he didn't want to go all the way up to his fourth-floor apartment to get something to eat.

Jerry asked Brian to go into his apartment and make him a sandwich. Brian answered, "Okay. Would a cheese sandwich be all right?"

"Fine" Jerry said.

James 3:8 (NASB) ... "But no one can tame the tongue; it is a restless evil and full of deadly poison."

Brian came out a few minutes later with Jerry's sandwich, and as Jerry started eating, Brian giggled under his breath. We all immediately knew Brian was up to something! Jerry was gobbling hungrily, not paying much attention to what he was eating. About halfway through his sandwich, Jerry said, "Brian, it tastes a little funny. How old is that cheese?"

"Mom just bought it yesterday," he responded.

Jerry kept eating.

At last, Brian couldn't contain his laughter any longer and burst out laughing.

Jerry looked up at him with a question in his eyes. "What?" he asked in a slightly frightened tone.

When Brian was able to stop laughing, he told us he sprayed Jerry's sandwich with RAID bug spray. We all started laughing, as Jerry ran up the stairs to his apartment to wash out his mouth, hoping he wasn't going to die from eating poison.

Proverbs 26:19 (ESV) ... "Is the man who deceives his neighbor and says, 'I am only joking!' "

Whenever one of the gang pulled a prank or played a joke on someone, we all had a good laugh. And when it was over, it was over! We promptly forgot about it. No one held a grudge or stayed angry, but all the same, you knew you should expect some appropriate revenge in the future.

We were still laughing about Jerry's lunch, when Brian lifted a screwdriver from his back pocket, walked over to the building entrance and perused the large glass panes inside the metal frame of each door. He had noticed that the windows were held in the door frames with nothing but a few screws. Brian tampered with the door closest to where we were sitting, explaining that if we took the screws out of the frame, the window would only rest in the frame with nothing to hold it in place.

One touch would cause the window to fall out of the frame and come crashing down onto the floor.

Proverbs 7:26 (NIV) ... "Many are the victims she has brought down; her slain are a mighty throng."

These windows were quite large, and when people walked through the door, they would typically push on the pane to open the door. All Brian needed now was an unwitting victim!

Jerry came out of the elevator, and Brian nudged him through the door he had not rigged, leading him to the front of the building. He convinced Jerry to race him from the bottom of the hill to the inside of the building lobby, intending for Jerry to run through the door with the missing screws. The race started, and the rest of us were inside the lobby, watching, waiting and laughing.

We watched Jerry, knowing what was about to happen. Jerry ran at full speed, rushing to the door to beat Brian in the preordained outcome. He reached out his hand to push on the window and open the door.

Isaiah 60:8 (ESV) … "Who are these that fly like a cloud, and like doves to their windows?"

The glass flew out of the door and exploded onto the floor, as Jerry followed, flying through the opening where the window had once been and landed on the lobby floor. The Lobby Crew erupted into gales of laughter, rolling on the floor with elation. The noise was so loud that everyone who lived on the first floor, including my family, came running out of their apartments to see what had happened.

Jerry was lying in the middle of a pile of shredded glass, looking like a superhero who had intentionally crashed through the window to save the day. Jerry got up gingerly, rattled, with glass stuck to his arms and legs. Fortunately, he was not hurt, only a little shaken.

The adults in the lobby started yelling at him, thinking he had done it on purpose. We joined in yelling at Jerry, accusing him of being a bad apple, and encouraging the crowd to think Jerry was at fault.

He tried to explain in vain, but no one would listen or believe him. Jerry was totally frustrated. He ran up the stairs to his apartment with tears in his eyes. We did not feel guilty in the least. The incident was a riot to watch. Still, there was one thing that Brian had not anticipated. Now that the window was broken, the lobby was freezing, and we couldn't hang out there until the door was fixed.

ST. JOHN'S AND THE "BIZARRE"

▲ ▲ ▲

1 CORINTHIANS 6:20 (ESV) ... "for you were bought with a price. So glorify God in your body."

One thing had not changed in our house: we still had to attend church on Sundays. We continued to use the routine of one of us going inside to get the church bulletin, in hopes of fooling Dad into thinking we had actually attended the service.

One Sunday, Gumby asked Billy and me if he could have our church money, and for some inexplicable reason, we gave it to him. We walked to the store, and Gumby went in while we waited outside. When he came back, he didn't have any candy. Instead, he had bought cigars! "What in the world was this all about?"

"It's really cool to smoke them, and these cigars have plastic tips on them that you can chew," he explained.

We were always primed for a challenge, so there we stood in front of the store—a bunch of stupid kids, puffing away on cigars. Gumby warned us not to inhale or we would get sick.

Being a man of adventure, of course I had to test this theory. I inhaled, turned blue, and became nauseous. I could now say with authority that inhaling cigars made you sick. I was no longer the gullible kid I had been. I had to find out things for myself now. I wasn't satisfied to listen to someone else's stories or opinions.

As Billy and I came into the house with our smudge faces on, we rolled into the back bedroom handing Dad the church bulletin. After quizzing Dad about what he was watching on television and making some small talk, we told Dad that Gumby was in the hall waiting for us. "We'll be back later."

Dad had a strange look on his face as he said, "Boys, tell Gumby you won't be coming back out."

We spoke with Gumby and told him we weren't coming back out.

"Why?"

We looked at each other with an unexplainable fear that something was wrong. We shrugged our shoulders and went back inside our apartment.

Standing in front of Dad in the back bedroom like two soldiers at attention, he asked us to move a little closer to him. We both took a step closer, and he motioned for us to move even closer. Our minds were now racing with fear, knowing we were just about to hear some bad news from Dad.

I was just a little closer to Dad than Billy was, and he took hold of my shirt and lifted it to his nose. "Smoking, huh?!"

Expecting to feel the full brunt of his anger, he quietly told us to go into the living room and wait for him. Tears filled our eyes from fear. Dad walked into the living room and had us sit on the couch. As we sat, Dad dropped a carton of cigarettes onto Billy's lap and said, "Start smoking."

Our minds were now racing with confusion as Dad handed Billy a pack of matches.

"But Dad, we don't want to smoke," we protested.

Dad merely replied, "If you finish just one pack, I'll give you permission to smoke."

Billy's demeanor had now changed from fear to pride as he kicked back, even crossing his legs up on the tabletop while striking a match to light up a cigarette hanging from his lips.

I was horrified as Billy boldly blew smoke circles out into the living room. Dad told me to light up, and I still protested as he placed a cigarette in my mouth and lit it. Halfway through my cigarette, tears were streaming from my eyes more from embarrassment than fear. Meanwhile, Billy was on his second cigarette and proud as can be when Dad told me I could stop.

Now as if watching a television show, I sat there along with my brothers and sisters watching Billy smoke his brains out. After about four cigarettes, Billy looked blue and a little sick, but he just kept on smoking. His formerly wide smile had now been replaced with only half a smile, and both legs had been placed firmly on the floor. Gone were the circles of smoke and his proud look. He was about to light up cigarette number six when he just exploded into tears, wailing about how sick he was. "I can't smoke anymore," he wailed, begging Dad to let him stop.

The marathon ended as Billy almost passed out on the couch, and Dad giving a ten-minute lecture on the dangers of smoking.

Proverbs 9:9 (NASB) … "Give instruction to a wise man, and he will be still wiser, Teach a righteous man, and he will increase in learning."

The public school students who were making their confirmation in the Catholic church had to go to classes on Wednesdays. We were allowed to leave school early to attend those classes at the St. John Vianney Catholic School. We normally got out of school at

3:00, but the administration of P.S. 138 would let us leave at 1:45 on Wednesdays to get to St John's by 2:00 p.m. for the one-hour class. Of course, we were always late to class because we would stop in the lots after being distracted by one thing or another.

This particular day the distraction was a squirrel. Whenever we would spot a squirrel, we would chase it and fling rocks at it. We had one squirrel trapped in a tree, slinging rocks at it with no success. I decided to climb up the tree to get better aim and distance. I had one rock in each hand. Halfway up the tree, my shirt caught hold of a branch sticking out, ripped off a few buttons and scratched my belly up pretty good.

I stubbornly continued up the tree, ignoring the stains of blood seeping through my shirt as I spotted the squirrel sitting on the top branch. I noticed the squirrel was now staring at me, and it turned into a contest as I gazed right back at him. It was as if he was instigating me to come further up the tree.

I was now starting to get quite nervous being all alone on the treetop with just me and my squirrel "friend." As I threw both rocks, the first bounced off the branch just next to him, and the second rock went whizzing just past his head. I was now defenseless, and my squirrel friend looked pretty angry at me. With one swoop, the squirrel screamed toward me.

I was now in an all-out fear attack, struggling to hold onto the tree branches. As he came closer, running across my back and down my leg, I could feel the tree jolting all the way to the bottom. As I watched from the treetop, he scurried straight toward the guys, and they all took off running straight to St. John's!

Making my way down the tree, I realized the guys who helped me get up to the first branch would no longer be there, leaving me with a seven-foot drop between the last branch and the ground. I looked frantically around to see if anyone was in sight to help me out of the tree with no luck. I sat on that lowest tree branch for ten minutes, calculating the seven-foot drop.

I then realized how late I was for school and began to work my way down. I hugged the tree trunk with my arms outstretched, wrapping around the bark and scraping my arms with my legs barely holding on. I was halfway down the tree trunk before losing my grip and falling the remaining four feet onto my back.

Lying on my back, looking up at the sky, all I could think of was the embarrassment of walking into the classroom, hearing the laughter from the guys, and the punishment ahead of me from the nun.

Luke 6:29 (NIV) … "If someone slaps you on one cheek, turn to them the other also. If someone takes your coat, do not withhold your shirt from them."

Sister John was our nun and the teacher of our confirmation classes. She was one mean old sister! When she caught me talking in class, she would walk straight over to me and slap me in the back of the head with all her might. If anyone laughed, she would slap them too! She was fairly old, and she couldn't hit all that hard—even if she tried. Still, you had to play along, pretending that she had hurt you because if she didn't think the punishment had sunk in, she would smack you with a ruler. And that certainly did hurt!

After making my way through the school lobby, I stood outside my classroom, peeking through the door window and trying to find the courage to go into the classroom. I quietly pushed opened the door and tried to unsuspectingly make it to my desk unnoticed. I was called to the front of the classroom and stood straight up while silently looking down at the floor when she suddenly asked, "Did you catch the squirrel?"

Apparently everyone had a good laugh at my adventure except me.

Then with her ruler, Sister John pointed and poked at my blood-stained shirt with three buttons missing, asking as she poked, "Does this hurt?"

As the words "No" we're leaving my lips, she smacked me straight across the belly, asking again, "Now does this hurt?"

"Yes, very much," I grimaced. A few more whacks with the ruler and a one-hour detention after school was fine with me. I just wanted to sit back down and soak in self-pity about my public humiliation.

1 Corinthians 11:18 (ESV) ... "For, in the first place, when you come together as a church, I hear that there are divisions among you. And I believe it in part."

Brian, Gumby, Tommy T, Matthew and a bunch of other guys went to school full-time at St. John Vianney's, so they were used to getting hit by the nuns every day. They would tell us stories about the cruelty of the sisters, and our eyes would widen in disbelief. We didn't go to St. John's full-time, although Dad probably thought that Catholic school would be better for us than public school. Catholic school was expensive, and Dad had too many kids to send, so P.S. 138 was good enough for us. Years later, our youngest sister, Peggy, did attend St. John's, but we didn't hold it against her.

Proverbs 1:10 (NIV)... "My son, if sinful men entice you, do not give in to them."

We didn't mind public school at all! We were off on Catholic holidays because we were Catholic, and we were off on Jewish holidays because public schools closed on those holidays. We also got off St. Patrick's Day because we were Irish; it was a pretty good deal.

One year, the public school teachers went on strike, which seemed to last for about two months. Every day, we would run screaming up to the windows of St. John's, laughing at our friends in the classrooms because they still had to go to school. St. John's school was only two stories high, so they could definitely hear us hollering outside of their windows.

Proverbs 24:16 (KJV) ... "For a just man falleth seven times, and riseth up again: but the wicked shall fall into mischief."

One day during the school strike, we were screaming outside of the school window, and the teacher left the room. Matthew, Tommy T., Gumby and Brian stuck their heads out of the window, wisecracking about being in "prison."

Billy and I stood beneath the window, with some other public school kids, yelling for them to make a break for it. "Jump from the window!" we yelled.

When they wouldn't jump, we hurled "chicken" (having no guts) insults at them. Finally, Tommy T. couldn't take the insults any longer. He climbed out of the window, hung onto the ledge, and jumped. He landed on his feet first, fell to the ground in a heap, and rolled on the grass. We helped him to his feet and he walked around for a minute, limping a little, but none the worse for the wear.

Matthew 15:14 (ESV) ... "Let them alone; they are blind guides. And if the blind lead the blind, both will fall into a pit."

When he had recovered, he called up to the window, daring the others to jump. It didn't take much encouragement. Matthew was next and then Gumby. Brian looked down at us, gauging his chances. He had just about gotten through the window, when we heard the voice of their teacher, Mr. Frank, scream from inside the classroom.

Without hanging onto the ledge, Brian leaped off, feet flying, arms waggling. We broke his fall when he landed on top of us, and we tumbled in a pile, laughing and rolling on the grass. Mr. Frank poked his head out the window, craning his neck to look down at us, and began screaming at the boys who had jumped. He demanded that they come back upstairs, at once!

We screamed back that he would jump down too if he was any kind of a man. Needless to say, he wouldn't jump, but we knew he'd be on us soon if we didn't get out of there. We ran towards our building, tossing insults back over our shoulders, as Mr. Frank hung out the window, yelling for all he was worth.

Proverbs 15:18 (ESV) ... "A hot-tempered man stirs up strife, but he who is slow to anger quiets contention."

The next day, the boys who jumped out of the window had to see the school principal, and they were placed on detention, meaning they had to stay after school for two hours, and they had to complete some kind of assignment during that time.

Later that same day, we were standing in front of our building, listening to Matthew tell us the story of what had happened when they went back to school. "Mr. Frank beat Brian with a ruler, and Brian just sat there and took it."

To validate Matthew's story, Brian showed us the marks from the ruler, and Billy started to harass him about letting Mr. Frank get away with it. Billy said, "Brian, you shouldn't have let Mr. Frank get away with that."

Billy was so convincing in his argument that it was as if we all became possessed with what Mr. Frank had done to Brian. As we listened to Billy talk, we got angrier and angrier. We started walking toward St. John's, whipped into a fury by Billy's eloquent speech.

Leviticus 19:18 (ESV) ... "You shall not take vengeance, nor bear any grudge against the sons of your people, but you shall love your neighbor as yourself; I am the LORD."

Matthew said, "I know which car belongs to Mr. Frank," and that was all we needed to hear. Within minutes, Mr. Frank's car had four flats, broken mirrors, and a cracked windshield. We put dirt in the gas tank and made long knife scratches on both sides of his car.

This, we hoped, would send a message about his physical abuse on our friend Brian!

The next day, Mr. Frank told the class about his car and how much trouble the culprit was in for the damage. The report that I heard was that Brian looked Mr. Frank right in the eye and said, "We also know where you live."

I shook my head when I heard this, figuring Brian was done for. He was certain to be kicked out of school for threatening his teacher. But, Mr. Frank decided to quit before we damaged his house too. He befriended Brian and his group of friends, and we got along just fine for the rest of the school year.

Ecclesiastes 2:24 (ESV) ... "There is nothing better for a person than that he should eat and drink and find enjoyment in his toil. This also, I saw, is from the hand of God."

Every year St. John's held a bazaar in the school yard. They had a Ferris wheel and lots of other rides, and game booths where the participants could win prizes like stuffed animals, dishes and money.

Everyone looked forward to the bazaar. We didn't have much organized entertainment in our neighborhood, and this bazaar was a two-weekend venture when the community could come together and enjoy some innocent festivities.

I had a serious misunderstanding of the word *bazaar* for a long time. I always pictured the two-week event as "bizarre," thinking it was meant to be a crazy, weird, freakish place. The Ferris wheel, which seemed gigantic to me, only enhanced the word "bizarre" in my mind. We would always watch the carnival crew put the gigantic wheel together, and I stood in fascinated wonder, as it took shape before my eyes.

The "bizarre" opened at 3:00 in the afternoon, and we would be the first in line to stand at the gate, waiting for it to open. When the gates opened, we ran straight to the Ferris wheel. I would ride the big wheel even though I was scared to death at the top of the ride. The attendant would stop the wheel to let riders off on the bottom while we were left hanging high above, staring way down at the ground.

Haggai 2:7 (NIV) ... " 'I will shake all nations, and what is desired by all nations will come, and I will fill this house with glory,' says the LORD Almighty."

When this happened, Billy would shake our basket back and forth, rocking us until I screamed for him to stop. Every year, I was sure I would die in a tragic fall, and every year I got off the ride without a scratch, with my mouth dry and my hands clammy, feeling exhilarated. From the spot at the very top of the Ferris wheel, you could look way off into the distance and see the whole group of buildings that made up the projects. At night, they were lit up like a fairy land in the twilight, and it was hard to believe we lived in such a distant place.

Beneath our dangling feet, the crowds looked like little ants, running back and forth. Billy always brought eggs to throw down onto the unsuspecting patrons, and he would cackle as they landed with a crunch and a splat far below.

Psalm 18:39 NASB) ... "For You have girded me with strength for battle; You have subdued under me those who rose up against me."

After we got off the Ferris wheel, we'd walk around the "bizarre," looking for trouble. Tommy and Matthew always tried to get me to start trouble with kids from other neighborhoods. My job was to bump and push into them. Because I was small, they would usually just push me away.

Once we had our targets in sight, Tommy T., Matthew, and a hand full other guys would blend into the crowd unnoticed, appearing not to have any relationship with me. I was sent in as a decoy to clash and start the action. The guys targeted were much bigger than I was, but I had a job to do, and I took it seriously.

On this particular outing, I bumped and pushed two big guys and they, in turn, threw me to the ground. Tommy T. and Matthew came running over to ask me what had happened as if they innocently became aware of an injustice.

Joel 2:11 (NIV) ... "The LORD thunders at the head of his army; his forces are beyond number, and mighty is the army that obeys his command. The day of the LORD is great; it is dreadful. Who can endure it?"

As if reading from a script, the guys told Tommy T. and Matthew to shut up and mind their business, and that was exactly the answer they were looking for. Tommy T. instructed the bullies to step outside of the grounds of the "bizarre" so they could fight. They laughed and followed us off the grounds for the obligatory fight.

We couldn't battle inside the "bizarre" because they had security, but once we were outside, all bets were off. The guys had fallen into the trap. They saw ten or so more guys quickly file in behind Tommy and realized what they had gotten themselves into.

A quick apology was made for pushing me, and Tommy T. accepted the apology, and then summarily grabbed him by his collar, but he shook loose. His friend immediately took off running, and the bully followed, taking off like a race horse. About two blocks away, they got caught.

Psalm 113:7 (NLT) … "He lifts the poor from the dust and the needy from the garbage dump."

I don't know what neighborhood these guys had come from, but they must have been sorry they were visiting the "bizarre." Matters quickly got ugly as both were slammed and plummeted to the ground. Then the guys were dragged across the street to the back of the Big Apple Supermarket. After being shoved and roughed up for quite a while, there was only one thing left.

The supermarket had large smelly garbage containers used to dump spoiled and rotten fruit, meats and vegetables. Sometimes at night we would walk over behind the supermarket to have target practice throwing rocks and bottles at the large rats that would feast inside the containers. After several more apologies, the guys were lifted and dumped head first into the dumpster while we laughed, and they cried out in panic. "Don't come out until we say so," they were instructed. If their heads appeared outside of the container, they would be bombarded with rocks and bottles.

We would wait quietly until they believed we had gone, and sure enough, they lifted the lid. Of course we had to respond, and they experienced a barrage of rocks and bottles. We would play this game for an hour or so, and then we would quietly walk away without their knowing whether or not we were still there.

Lamentations 3:7 (CEV) ... "God built a fence around me that I cannot climb over, and he chained me down."

Eventually, St. John's started to charge a nominal admission fee, just to keep the undesirable element out, and that included us! However, that gigantic fence enclosing the "bizarre" couldn't keep us out even though we didn't have the money to get in. We would hop, go under, or just clip the fence somewhere in a deserted location and find our way in. We would go on to taunt and harass all those in charge of trying to keep us out.

The security for the "bizarre" was comprised of five to seven very large men who acted like Mafia hit men, drank a copious amount of beer, and liked to gamble inside of the school as the "bizarre" was going on. When they were called on to deal with the likes of us, we would harass them to the point they would almost get physical.

One night, as they circled the "bizarre," rounding us up to kick us off the property, Tommy T. was so upset it took almost all of them to get him off the property. The "bizarre" was set up with a large gated fence around the entire property with an entrance on the Castle Hill Avenue side and another entrance on the Seward Avenue side. The Castle Hill side entrance was where people paid the entry fee. A table was set up, and only one or two people at a time could fit though after payment. The Seward Avenue side was a large two-gate exit that opened at the end of each night, allowing thirty to fifty people to pass through as the crowd would swarm out at the end of each night.

One night, after being kicked out by the Mafia guys, we tried to come up with a way to get back at them. Brian took off running across Seward Avenue, down the grass hill, and into the side of our building. After several minutes he bolted out of the building, back up the grass hill, and across Seward Avenue holding a lock and chain. As he was wrapping the two poles of the gate together, he laughed with delight, saying, "If we can't get in there, they aren't getting out!"

We waited until closing and watched as people came to the closed gate frustrated about not being able to leave out of that exit. All of their frustration was taken out on the Mafia guys as we watched them being yelled at and shoved around by the now rude and unruly crowd. Tension went on for years between the make-believe Mafia guys and the gang.

MOM'S "LITTLE PROBLEM"

▲ ▲ ▲

PROVERBS 31:10 (NASB) … "AN excellent wife, who can find? For her worth is far above jewels."

Robbie and his neighbor, Kevin, lived on the tenth floor. The youngest of five kids, Kevin had two older sisters and two older brothers. Kevin's mom was a very nice lady whom everyone liked—even the kids. She always said "Hello" and talked to us. She would ask us questions about school and how the family was doing and, unlike most grownups, she seemed genuinely interested in our answers. Kevin's mom had a job outside the home, and every day she would leave the building and head to the bus stop on Castle Hill Avenue, where she would catch the bus to go to work. One day, we were walking toward the stores when we heard sirens blaring and saw an ambulance and police car racing down Castle Hill Avenue.

James 4:14 (ESV)… "yet you do not know what tomorrow will bring. What is your life? For you are a mist that appears for a little time and then vanishes."

This was a very sad day in our neighborhood. Apparently, a car had lost control and had slammed into the bus stop—the very one where

Kevin's mom waited every morning. The car struck Kevin's mom and sent her flying high into the air. She landed so far away that it was hard to believe she had been standing at the bus stop only moments before.

Within minutes, the area looked like a crime scene with yellow tape everywhere, fire engines, police cars, ambulances and mobs of people watching. Throughout the years, this same scenario would happen several times a year. Castle Hill was a four-lane street and a dangerous one to cross. We watched fidgeting, unsure of what to say or how to act, watching as Kevin's mom lay unconscious with a pool of blood spreading out from her body on the pavement. Kevin's mom had beautiful blonde hair, and I always used to look at it in awe whenever I saw her. Now, with her body lying broken on the pavement, her blonde hair became soaked with blood, like a sponge absorbing every drop, until there was nothing to be seen but red strands.

I'll never forget that image nor the feeling of complete helplessness as we watched the attendants carry her away in the ambulance. She spent a full year in the hospital and was never quite the same after that day. Back then, in our projects, it seemed like every family had its own sad tragedies to handle. And our family was no different.

Judges 5:28 (NASB) … "Out of the window she looked and lamented, the mother of Sisera through the lattice, 'Why does his chariot delay in coming? Why do the hoofbeats of his chariots tarry?'"

Stickball is played with a broomstick and a pink Spaulding rubber ball—a type of ball still sold today in many parts of New York City. We played this game on the grass near the side of the building. From the sewer cap in the grass, which we considered home plate, to our building was roughly a hundred feet. From home plate, you could look directly at our apartment. Eleven of our windows faced the field plus, three around the corner faced Castle Hill Avenue.

On Saturday mornings, we had to clean our apartment from top to bottom, and the person assigned to the window detail would cry like a baby. Dad assigned everyone a house-cleaning duty, and mine was the smaller of the two bathrooms. This minor task was so envied, I became the brunt of insulting jokes by my siblings.

Mark 9:26 (NASB) ... "After crying out and throwing him into terrible convulsions, it came out; and the boy became so much like a corpse that most of them said, 'He is dead!' "

This particular day was beautiful, and we couldn't wait to get outside to play ball. The sky was bright blue—so bright it hurt your eyes to look up. Not a cloud was in the sky. We were all feeling pretty good, kidding each other and laughing as we were about to start the game.

Eddie was the lead-off hitter. The batter would bounce the ball on the sewer cap. After two or three bounces, he would swing the broomstick, sending a "swishing" sound that everyone loved to hear. Hopefully, the pink Spaulding skyrocketed into the air. But sometimes, it was "a swing and a miss" that just caused a draft. Eddie dropped his ball on the sewer cap, and it bounced once, twice, three, four times until there were no more bounces, and the ball slowly rolled into the grass. Eddie stood there frozen, and we all yelled and laughed at his antics. Eddie then dropped his broomstick, turned, and started to walk towards Seward Avenue as if he was a robot.

His brother, Bone, yelled out, "He's having a convulsion!"

I was unaware of what a "convulsion" was as I watched his eyes rolling back and forth. Bone desperately shoved his hand toward Eddie's face. Then he stuck his hand into Eddie's mouth to pull his tongue back so he would not choke on it.

We carried Eddie to the elevator and into his house where his parents took control of the situation. Thirty minutes later, Eddie was given the green light to head back downstairs and continue the game. I now understood about "convulsions," and learned that the main thing to do in such situations was not to let Eddie swallow his tongue.

Psalm 18:4 (NASB) ... "The cords of death encompassed me, And the torrents of ungodliness terrified me."

Eddie was back at home plate. I watched from the outfield, which was only a few feet from our kitchen window. As he got ready, and the ball was bouncing on the sewer cap, I could see him timing the bounce, focusing, watching.

Suddenly, I heard a loud exploding crash from behind me. I turned and saw a pressing iron dangling from our apartment window by its cord; the window glass shattered into hundreds of pieces on the grass below. I watched with fascination and bewilderment as the cord began to snake back into the window, the iron bobbing slowly, crawling up against the wall toward the sill.

Now I could hear loud eerie screams coming from our apartment. The iron disappeared into the window and then crashed through the next window, shattering the glass and hanging below the sill from the cord. Crash!

By now, the stickball game had stopped. Everyone on the field stood watching as my mom systematically shattered all of the living room windows in our apartment.

Deuteronomy 29:28 (NIV) ... "In furious anger and in great wrath the **LORD** *uprooted them from their land and thrust them into another land, as it is now."*

One by one, each window was smashed as the iron was thrown through the glass. The iron dangled below the sill until slowly and methodically it was drawn back into the apartment to disappear until it was thrown through the next window. Glass was flying everywhere, and the loud eerie screaming continued until I thought my head would explode.

Now in panic mode, I ran into the building, down the hallway as fast as I could, and into our apartment. Once inside, I saw Mom screaming at the top of her lungs with Alice and Tommy trying to stop her rampage. It wasn't long before the police and the ambulance arrived, and Mom was on her way back to the hospital mental ward.

Deuteronomy 28:34 (NASB) ... "You shall be driven mad by the sight of what you see."

Being an alcoholic at that time was considered a mental disorder worthy of a stay in the psychiatric ward of the hospital. So that's where Mom usually ended up. We would visit her at Jacobi Hospital's mental ward, and if any of the other patients came near us, she would scream at them to get away, protecting us like a fierce lioness.

She didn't have a mental problem, not in the same sense that many of the other patients in the psychiatric ward did. She had a drinking problem. But she was, nevertheless, staying in the same ward as patients with severe mental and behavioral problems.

One afternoon while visiting, Mom left to go back to her room. We waited for the guard to unlock the heavy armored looking door with one of the many skeleton keys attached to a large circular key ring. Jokingly, as the guard was on the other side unlocking the door, my brother, Michael, pushed me out of the door area. Michael, along with other siblings, slipped out the door without the guard's noticing I was still inside.

As I banged furiously on the door and watched my siblings and the guard pass through another door, I could see Michael and the others laughing. I was panicking as I looked through the small thick glass door window, realizing now I was alone and on my own. I turned around, and a woman and two men were standing and staring at me. I was stuck with no way out as I looked around for an attendant or guard for help, but none was around. The woman put her arm around me, and the two men began to utter strange sounds as they rubbed my head and touched my face. I was not sure if I should run around the room or just go along with these folks, remembering Mom said they were harmless.

Nevertheless, I was trembling and frozen with fear. Suddenly, from across the room, I heard the loudest screech I have ever heard in my life. "GET THE HELL AWAY FROM HIM!" Mom dashed across the room, shoving the two men and the lady, sending them running off into different corners of the room. Mom (who I now thought was "Superwoman") asked, "Are you okay?" Knowing I was fine and hearing about the prank pulled by my siblings, Mom giggled as she had a guard to take me downstairs safely.

Coming out of the building, Michael laughed wildly as I told them what "Superwoman" had done to those three other patients. After that little prank, I made sure I was always the first out the door when leaving the hospital.

Ephesians 5:4 (NIV) … "Nor should there be obscenity, foolish talk or coarse joking, which are out of place, but rather thanksgiving."

Most kids have an innate sense of boundaries when it comes to the things they can joke about and the things they should leave alone. Most of my friends didn't make fun of my mom and her little problem. When she was home and feeling well, she always treated my friends as if they were her own, and they thought that was cool. We would joke about each other's moms sometimes, but always in such a way that it wasn't mean or cruel.

My theory was tested full force as I was just back from the lots, heading to the front of the stores. For some reason, I had this eerie feeling that I was being watched. Noticing whispers with long stares at me, I couldn't shake the feeling and just knew something wasn't right. I checked myself up and down. "Is my zipper open?" "Is my shirt on backward?" "Did I rub my dirty hands across my face, leaving me to look like a mutt dog?"

As I walked into the house, there were pitiful looks from my siblings along with silence. Mom had managed to outdo herself this time. After drinking most of the morning, she decided she needed some more beer. As she was halfway across Castle Hill Avenue, a very nice lady from building 2140 dashed across the street as she simultaneously jerked around trying desperately to get her coat off and cover Mom, who was standing like a frozen statue completely naked in the middle of the street.

How Mom managed to make it from our building to the middle of Castle Hill Avenue completely naked still baffles me. Most of our moms had one kind of problem or another, and we all knew the feeling of hurt and shame that went along with those problems. So jokes about moms were considered in bad taste.

If it wasn't that a kid's mom had a drinking problem, it was likely that the father drank too much or beat his wife or kids. Divorces weren't common or well-accepted in those days, and most families simply stuck it out. The first time I ever heard of a divorce was when

Gumby's parents split up. At the time, I really couldn't understand what was happening. I thought Gumby's parents were both great, and that they got along well. The divorce was really hard on Gumby because he was the oldest son with one younger brother and three younger sisters.

"RUN! IT'S THE COPS!"

▲ ▲ ▲

1 Corinthians 3:2 (NIV) … "I gave you milk, not solid food, for you were not yet ready for it. Indeed, you are still not ready."

On days when we had no school, Gumby would bang on our door for us to come out and help him find something to do. That invitation usually meant trouble! Today our targeted location was the milk factory area down near the Sanitation Department where Dad worked. The milk factory delivered milk to all the neighborhoods. The boxy-looking trucks used for deliveries were parked in the factory parking lot.

Across from the milk factory was a house that had apple and plum trees along with grapevines. We'd hop the fence, grab as much fruit as we could, then hop back out onto the street before someone caught us. Our biggest nemesis was the house owner's Doberman pinscher who was as mean as any dog we ever knew.

The walk to the milk factory from our apartment took about twenty minutes. On this particular day, we were headed in the general direction of the factory when Gumby announced, "I'm thirsty. Let's stop at the milk factory to see if we can get something to drink." Once we arrived at the milk factory, we could easily peek inside and see the conveyor belts circling the inside of the factory loading the containers with milk or juice.

We poked our heads into the door, getting ready to grab some orange juice when from behind, the three of us in perfect harmony were shoved into the doorway and thrown onto the floor by a very large factory worker. We scattered in different directions running to escape, each of us on our own trying to get out of there. We began laughing at the guy we nicknamed "Lurch" who had swatted us to the floor in a single swipe.

We gathered across the street in front of the house with the fruit trees. Our attention now turned to grabbing some fruit before moving on. Our only problem was the Doberman pinscher prowling in the yard. Our technique for getting some of the fruit out of the yard was for one of us to go to the other end of the fence and keep the dog occupied by kicking the bottom of the fence.

Gumby was appointed the kicker this time, I was nominated to jump over the fence for the fruit, and Billy was designated as the lookout and helper to get me over the fence. As Gumby kicked and I hopped, Billy shouted out his order for fruit as if he was sitting at a restaurant. I realized that the Doberman pinscher was racing straight toward me. Gumby was now yelling for me to run, and Billy merely laughed at my predicament.

I stuffed a few apples into my pockets and leaped onto the top of the fence. I thought I was in the clear, needing only to jump off the fence top, but my sneaker and the bottom of my dungarees got caught and tangled in the fence. I jumped anyway, hoping against hope that my weight would pull me off the fence. No such luck! I was left dangling with the Doberman pinscher chewing at my sneaker, and Billy and Gumby desperately trying to get my leg loose.

After a few good tugs, I came crashing to the ground with Billy and Gumby falling backward. Getting up, I reached into my pocket and tossed Gumby and Billy one of the apples I managed to hold onto as a thank you.

While biting into his apple, Gumby stubbornly shouted, "I still want some orange juice!" He figured we could steal some juice out of the parked milk trucks, but to do that, we had to head to the back of their parking lot in the far corner next to the Sanitation Department and climb over the fence.

Leviticus 14:41 (NLT) … Next the inside walls of the entire house must be scraped thoroughly and the scrapings dumped in the unclean place outside the town."

I was scared, but Billy and Gumby declared everything would be fine. We would hop over the fence, grab some juice, and get back out. Billy went first, climbing quickly over the fence. As Gumby was helping me over, Billy loudly whispered to be careful because there was barbed wire on top.

"What's barbed wire?" I asked innocently.

Billy said, "You'll find out if it sticks you!"

"Be careful," Gumby warned.

Sure enough, as Gumby helped me up and I began to climb over the fence, I got caught on the top in the barbed wire, and my pants ripped all the way down the leg. I screamed loudly, falling over the fence, my pants leg shredded.

Now in the parking lot, I surveyed the damage and discovered that I had a nasty scrape from my knee to my ankle where the wire had grabbed my leg.

"Are you all right?" Billy asked.

"No, I'm not. I'm bleeding, and it hurts like heck!"

"Oh, you'll be fine," offered Gumby as he jumped up and over the fence with no problem.

I stood up and jumped back onto the fence to make my way back over, figuring I'd get out of there and just head home.

Gumby and Billy each grabbed one of my legs, pulling me off the fence and insisting I had to stay.

At first, I thought I would bleed to death, but once the search for the orange juice started, I was preoccupied with the idea that we might get caught, and I forgot all about my injured leg.

Exodus 22:2 (NIV) … "If a thief is caught breaking in at night and is struck a fatal blow, the defender is not guilty of bloodshed."

We began to search the milk trucks for the distinctive orange juice made at that factory. Within minutes, Gumby whispered, "Hey, look! I found it!" meaning the cartons of orange juice.

I said, "I think we should just take what we have and get out of here before we get caught."Instead we clashed three quart containers together in celebration of our find. As Billy and Gumby chugged down the orange juice, I was getting cranky and complaining about my injured leg.

Then I saw Billy's eyes light up when he saw the keys had been left in the ignition of the truck.

I wanted out! I was now scared to death.

Billy wanted to go for a joyride.

I just stood there, saying, "No," again and again—like a robot.

Gumby yelled, "Get in, Johnny, and stop whining!"

We climbed up into the truck, and Billy turned the key. The engine rumbled to life, with Billy cackling over the noise. "Oh…this is going to be fun!"

Gumby protested. "Let me drive, Billy!"

"Wait until we get out of the parking lot."Gumby wasn't happy with Billy's answer, but he agreed.

I was in the back of the truck, drinking the orange juice and commenting on how delicious it was, having already forgotten about our illegal caper.

Billy started to drive toward the front of the milk factory entrance as the truck was pulling and bumping. We realized then that one of the back tires was flat. From the spot where we had stopped, we could see the loading dock and three guys standing there smoking cigarettes and laughing. We also noticed that one of the guys was "Lurch," the big guy who had shoved us through the doors inside the factory.

I was now in full panic mode after seeing Lurch, and without a hesitation, Billy whispered, "Look for another truck."

I cried out, "No! We are out of here!"

Billy won that argument too. We grabbed our orange juice and were off searching for another truck. We poked our heads into another truck, and sure enough, the keys hanging in the ignition called our names. As we rolled slowly inside the parking lot, we came into full view of the platform, and the three men were gone. The area was now deserted, so we slowly pulled out of the parking lot. No one was around, and now we were all laughing, albeit nervously.

Proverbs 16:18 (NIV) … "Pride goes before destruction, a haughty spirit before a fall."

Proud of our accomplishment, but feeling like we would be dragged off to jail at any moment, Billy took a right turn out of the parking lot and headed down the block toward the Sanitation Department that was on Zerega Avenue. We took a right turn onto Zerega Ave, a cobblestone street having uneven bricks, causing our ride to feel like a bumpy roller coaster.

All the while, Gumby and I were trying to stop the orange juice from being sprayed throughout the back of the truck.

"Billy, pull over and let me drive," Gumby begged, and surprisingly, Billy agreed. He was about to pull over so Gumby could slide into the driver's seat, when I looked out the back window of the truck and saw a police car about a block away headed in our direction.

I yelled, "The cops are behind us!"

My announcement sent Gumby and Billy into a panic, and I now felt very uneasy about our situation. Meanwhile, Billy was sticking his head out of the truck window, looking back to see the cops. As he did, the truck drifted into the oncoming lane. Gumby, noticing we were about to have a head-on collision, grabbed the steering wheel and swerved back into our lane as the other driver blasted his horn, sending us all into a double panic mode. Billy and Gumby were in a shouting match about what to do next.

2 Corinthians 11:33 (NIV) … "But I was lowered in a basket from a window in the wall and slipped through his hands."

The cops made a right-hand turn, heading up the block from where we had just come. Because they were headed toward the milk factory, we now assumed that the cops were on to us. Billy pulled over beside of the sanitation building, and the three of us jumped out of the truck, leaving the keys in the ignition with the engine still running. We ran behind the sanitation building.

The East River runs behind the Sanitation Department and then flows underneath the Union Port Bridge. The river continues behind the drive-in movie theater, where there is also a pier on the other side of the river. Our only escape from the cops now would be to swim across the river or hide in the rocks along the river bank.

Psalm 46:4 (NIV) … "There is a river whose streams make glad the city of God, the holy place where the Most High dwells."

Gumby ran to the front of the building and peeked cautiously around the side. "The cops still haven't come back down the block," which is what we thought they would do.

"Maybe they didn't know that we were driving the truck," Billy said, "But I don't trust them. Maybe it's a trap. What if they are waiting to catch us if we go back to the truck?"

Instead of doing anything, we just stood there with our hands jammed in our pants pockets, trying to figure out what to do next. We surely couldn't stay there hiding all night.

I noticed a square-shaped cement mixer near the riverbed and said out loud, "I bet that floats. Billy, help me get the mixer into the water." I was thinking we could float down to the drive-in movie theater.

We found that the mixer was heavy, and then we weren't sure if it would float.

Suddenly, Gumby yelled, "RATS!" Scampering between the rocks on the shore were four or five big river rats. Gumby grabbed some rocks and started throwing them at the now running rats. Once out of rocks, Gumby noticed one big scary looking momma rat, just standing on a rock staring at us.

Exodus 2:3 (NASB) … "But when she could hide him no longer, she got him a wicker basket and covered it over with tar and pitch. Then she put the child into it and set it among the reeds by the bank of the Nile."

We frantically pushed the mixer into the water, and sure enough, it floated. Billy said, "I wonder if we can all fit," and I answered, "I think we can. Gumby, grab something for oars," but he was too pre-occupied thinking about the rats.

Billy grabbed some tree branches and threw them into the mixer that we were now calling our "boat." We climbed into the square-shaped cement mixer and pushed away from the shore. Gumby yelled a goodbye to his rat "friend," and we floated slowly down the river. Gumby started to jokingly shake the boat, and I yelled, "Stop!" I was afraid we would tip over and drown.

2 Kings 6:6 (NIV) … "The man of God asked, 'Where did it fall?' When he showed him the place, Elisha cut a stick and threw it there, and made the iron float."

After a few minutes, we settled in for the journey, and I looked up at the sky, imagining we were pirates sailing on the high seas. I hollered, "Ahoy, mates," and started to laugh while Billy squealed about how cold the water was and how he hoped we didn't fall in.

We planned to float down the river a short way, under the Union Port Bridge to the drive-in where we would watch the featured movie—"Romeo and Juliet"—that was playing that night on the big screen. Billy and I had seen the movie a few nights before when we went with a bunch of our other friends. We had sneaked in through a hole in the back fence—the normal procedure to get in.

Suddenly, we heard a loud rumbling sound under the mixer and all around us. The water was violently splashing everywhere. I had no idea what was going on, and my mind had flashing thoughts of a gigantic sea monster about to swallow us whole.

Gumby yelled out, "Blues! Blues! Blues!" We had run smack into a school of bluefish, and as quick as they had hit us, they were gone, continuing their racket further upstream.

Acts 27:43 (NIV) … "But the centurion wanted to spare Paul's life and kept them from carrying out their plan. He ordered those who could swim to jump overboard first and get to land."

By now it was almost dark. I came out of my sea-monster nightmare and looked ahead to see the Union Port Bridge still quite a ways off. Gumby focusing behind us hissed, "What's that light?"

We peered into the dusk, and I saw clearly what was causing the light. I screamed: "Oh, no!" An oil tanker was headed straight toward us, and the steersman was oblivious to us. The ship was headed to the other side of the bridge to the Hess oil refinery. On the count of three, we jumped into the water and swam for our lives. We were all good swimmers, and even with the weight of our clothes, we managed to make good speed. Gumby was shouting, "I'm freezing!" and Billy retorted, "If you don't keep swimming, you'll be dead!

I started to panic because my shoes were getting heavier as they became saturated with water, and they were now dragging me down. "I don't think I can make it," I yelled.

Gumby and Billy swam back over and grabbed me, and we somehow made it safely to shore.

Acts 27:40 (NASB)… "And casting off the anchors, they left them in the sea while at the same time they were loosening the ropes of the rudders; and hoisting the foresail to the wind, they were heading for the beach."

Gasping for air in the cold evening breeze, we threw ourselves on the ground and watched as our cement mixer pirate ship was ploughed under by the gigantic tanker. We climbed up onto a rocky area at the side of the river, shivering, and watching the tanker pass us in slow motion. Gumby picked up a rock and threw it at the tanker, cursing it and the crew on board.

The three of us took turns throwing rocks, and I proudly noted that my rock hit the side of the tanker as it passed. By now, my eyes had adjusted to the dim light, and I could see the captain standing on the deck of the ship as it was slowly passing us. Billy tried hitting him with a rock, but he disappeared into a lower-level cabin.

Gumby called after him, proclaiming that he was a chicken and, no doubt, afraid of us. Just then, the captain emerged from below the deck. Gumby squinted into the dusk, asking what the captain was holding in his hand.

I heard Billy's gasp beside me as he identified the shape in the growing darkness. He screamed, "It's a rifle!"

Leviticus 2:13 (NASB) ... "Every grain offering of yours, moreover, you shall season with salt, so that the salt of the covenant of your God shall not be lacking from your grain offering; with all your offerings you shall offer salt."

As the captain pointed the rifle at us and started to shoot, we took off running, scrambling up the rocky slope on slippery feet. I fell to the ground screaming, "I've been hit!" and Gumby and Billy ran over to where I lay gasping in pain.

I had a vision of the old cowboy movies I used to watch with my dad. I imagined myself falling dead in the middle of a western street, and I knew I was going to die with the sound of the captain's rifle shot still ringing in my ears. Billy dropped down on his knees next to me. I was moaning, "My back, my back. I'm going to die."

Billy glanced over his shoulder at the tanker that had now passed us completely, and then he braced my back and sat me upright. He pulled off my shirt as I shivered, and Gumby ran down to the river and grabbed an old milk carton that had washed up on shore. He filled it with water and poured it on my back assuring me salt water was good for all types of cuts and bruises. "It was just a salt pellet gun," he said reassuringly. "You're not going to die."

Romans 3:16 (NIV) ... "ruin and misery mark their ways."

I wasn't so sure. I had no idea what a salt pellet gun was, but the bullets stung like a hundred bees. I was having a bad day. I had three sprained fingers from a game of tackle football the day before, I had scraped my leg from knee to ankle at the milk factory, and now my back was burning as if it was on fire.

Billy said, "We should get out of sight. Let's go into the woods up the slope. Gumby, is your lighter still working?"

He dug the lighter from his pocket to see if it still worked after being soaked in the river. He flicked it, and yep, it worked all right. The flame shot up from the lighter.

I said "Gumby, don't give Billy the lighter because I know he's up to no good."

Proverbs 13:20 (NASB) ... "He who walks with wise men will be wise, But the companion of fools will suffer harm."

Billy grabbed the lighter and headed off to find scraps of wood to make a campfire, while Gumby helped me up the rocky slope. Billy came back with some wood and got a fire going. The three of us sat on rocks in the glow, warming our feet and waiting for our clothes to dry. Billy got up and walked away, going deeper into the darkened woods.

"Gumby, where's Billy going?"

He just grinned and said, "He's looking for trouble."

I was hungry, cold and miserable, and I just wanted to go home. The only food I'd had all day was the fruit we picked from the yard near the factory and the orange juice from the milk truck. Gumby admitted that he was also starving. We discussed our next move: to go home or continue to the drive-in movie theater. Gumby insisted on the drive-in as I just shrugged my shoulders, sighed and said, "That's fine with me."

Proverbs 25:21 (CEB) ... "If your enemies are starving, feed them some bread; if they are thirsty, give them water to drink."

I knew the drive-in movie theater had plenty of great food at their snack bar, but we still had to get there. Gumby asked if I had any money, and I told him I didn't. I asked Gumby the same question, and he said he didn't. Gumby thought for a minute and then suggested that perhaps Billy had money. "Gumby, I'm fairly sure that Billy doesn't have any money either."

I assured him that if we could only get to the movie theater, I could steal something for us to eat. That idea was just fine with Gumby, and he decided we should get going right away.

I staggered to my feet, feeling sore and out of sorts, and then I heard a sound. I whimpered: "Now what's happening? I've had enough excitement for one day."

"It sounds like Billy squealing," Gumby replied. We stood near the fire, peering off into the dark trees until Billy emerged from the woods yelling for us to run. He screamed, "Let's get out of here!" We flew off in the direction of the Union Port Bridge.

Gumby and I shouted in harmony at Billy, "What happened? What happened?"

Luke 3:17 (NIV) ... "His winnowing fork is in his hand to clear his thresh-ing floor and to gather the wheat into his barn, but he will burn up the chaff with unquenchable fire."

We followed Billy, stumbling along on our hands and knees through the dark along the riverbed. "What happened?" I puffed, as we ran.

"I set the woods on fire, and it started to burn out of control!" Billy answered.

Gumby stopped and looked back in the direction of the campfire and beyond, where you could now see a lovely blaze, with smoke ris-ing into the night sky.

"What did you do?" Gumby muttered, shaking his head in be-wilderment. "Oh man, Billy! The fire trucks are coming."

We continued running toward the Union Port Bridge along the river. As we got to the bridge, we climbed up the side until we made it to the top. Running across the middle of the bridge span, we paused and watched the red lights from the fire trucks near the woods.

Hebrews 12:29 (KJV) ... "For our God is a consuming fire."

The fire was huge! As I watched the fire light up the night sky, I asked in wonder, "What did you set on fire, Billy?"

"I found a mattress with the stuffing hanging out of a hole. I didn't think it would go up in flames so quickly. It was like a bonfire once it got going, and the trees nearby also caught fire. Everything around me started burning!"

I couldn't quite tell if Billy was scared or proud of his accomplishment. We stood there for a few moments in a hushed awe, watching the fire grow with flames now high in the air. Gumby stood there with his hands jammed in his wet pockets, a stupid grin on his face, mumbling, "Now that's what I call a fire."

We started walking again, and I started bragging to Gumby that my brothers Michael and Tommy had jumped off this bridge. Suddenly, blaring alarms and bells were ringing all around us as a tugboat came down the river, and the drawbridge was about to open. We ran as fast as we could toward the end of the bridge as the wooden gates came down to prevent cars from passing. We could feel the bridge begin to lift below us as we ran and scurried under the wooden gates to safety.

Looking back toward the small cabin that housed the bridge workers (the guys in charge of lifting and lowering the bridge), we could see two men inside laughing hysterically as if they were playing a cat-and-mouse game, trying to lower the gates onto our heads.

1 Timothy 4:7 (HCSB)... "But have nothing to do with irreverent and silly myths. Rather, train yourself in godliness."

Exhausted from our sprint to get off the bridge, we stood and watched as the tugboat slowly passed under the bridge. Gumby said he'd heard that someone jumped off the bridge last year and landed right on the windshield of a speedboat.

I didn't believe it. "Really?" I asked cautiously. "Did he live?"

Gumby said the guy in the boat was so aggravated about his broken windshield that he picked up the kid and threw him into the river.

"Really?" I asked again.

"Really!" Gumby asserted with a knowing smile.

I said I would like to jump off this bridge someday. I wasn't all that sure about ever having the nerve, but I wasn't about to admit that.

Billy stopped and peered into the dark for a minute and then he said, "Look, I can see the movie from here. It's already started."

We sprinted across the four-lane highway and then a short distance to the back of the movie theater. We glanced to the other side of the river where we could see the oil tanker that almost drowned us. Looking at each other, thinking "revenge," we decided to just move forward.

Ezekiel 8:7 (NIV) … "Then he brought me to the entrance to the court. I looked, and I saw a hole in the wall."

As soon as we got inside, I planned to go straight to the snack bar. I was starving! Because I had been at the drive-in only a week earlier, I knew there wasn't much security. The drive-in theater had only an old, rickety wooden fence with holes every few feet surrounding the lot. Gumby popped his head into one of the many holes and looked from side to side. "Looks clear to me," he whispered.

Billy gave him a push from behind, and Gumby climbed through. One by one, we slipped through the hole and then made our way closer to the screen, searching for milk crates or something to sit on. Undesirables would often sneak into the drive-in to watch the shows and then leave the milk crates and boxes behind for the next group of renegades to use.

I found two crates, but we still needed another one. Gumby found the third crate, and we looked for a spot to sit in the middle of the lot—somewhere near the snack bar.

Isaiah 58:7 (NIV) … "Is it not to share your food with the hungry and to provide the poor wanderer with shelter—when you see the naked, to clothe them, and not to turn away from your own flesh and blood?"

We lined up our crates and made sure the speakers worked so we could hear the audio from the movie. Who needs a car when you can sit under the stars and watch the movie for free? The sound was cracked and brittle, booming out of the dented metal speaker. I told Gumby and Billy I would be right back, then sprinted to the snack bar. It was empty of customers, with only one young lady behind the cash register. These were definitely not the right conditions for a food heist. I turned around to leave, and then I heard the manager call the cashier into his office. This was my chance! I ducked down out of sight and crawled under the railing that separated me from the food. I looked to see that no one was watching, then reached up and grabbed two pizza boxes, and two hot dogs wrapped in silver foil. I stuffed the hot dogs under my damp shirt and juggling the pizza boxes, I crawled back under the railing and made my way to the door.

When I returned, Billy and Gumby were staring at the screen, laughing and whispering about the movie. I stood next to Billy and lifted my shirt, dropping the foil-wrapped hot dogs and pizza boxes in a pile on the ground.

"Wow!" Billy cheered. "That's great! How did you know I was hungry?"

Gumby and I started to laugh, remembering our conversation near the fire in the woods. Billy had been far away at the time, setting fire to a discarded mattress, but we figured he was as hungry as we were, so we didn't bother to ask.

Matthew 5:28 (ESV)... "But I say to you that everyone who looks at a woman with lustful intent has already committed adultery with her in his heart."

The three of us settled in under the stars, happy as pigs in mud, living the good life and loving every minute of it. We watched the movie, ate hot dogs and pizza. At that moment, I couldn't imagine anything better than this. Even wearing soggy clothes, weathering injuries, and rifle shots didn't dampen my spirits. I stared up at the screen, my heart swelling in my chest, and I said out loud, "I told you that Juliet was beautiful. Just look at her! Why does she have to die at the end?"

Gumby scowled. "Thanks a lot. You just told me the ending, and I haven't seen the movie yet.""Sorry, I forgot!"

Billy was thirsty so he asked me to go get some sodas. I told him I'd wait until intermission, when the snack bar was crowded. We watched the movie in silence for a few minutes, and then Billy noticed one of the cars near where we were sitting.

"Look at that car shaking," he said. "Let's go over there and knock on the window."

Gumby suggested we should peek in the window instead. We started walking toward the car.

1 John 1:9 (NIV) ... "If we confess our sins, he is faithful and just to forgive us our sins and to cleanse us from all unrighteousness."

Just as we were about to peek in the window, three big guys appeared, pulling out their police badges.

"Hold it right there, boys," one of them commanded.

I hollered frantically, "Run," but one of the cops pulled out his gun, pointed it right at me and said, "Go ahead. Run if you want!"

My knees went weak, and I stood still, staring into the barrel of his gun with dread. The policemen weren't wearing uniforms; they were dressed in plain clothes and had come out of nowhere, spoiling our fun as it was about to begin.

"You three are on private property, and you seem to be making a lot of trouble today. You're the same kids who took the milk truck on a joy ride and started the fire, right?"

We had no answer. Standing there soaked and forlorn, I thought it would be useless to deny the charges. We thought we'd gotten away without being seen during each of our escapades that day, but obviously that wasn't true. Seemingly someone had seen us at every turn, and the reports were flying.

I pictured the police department phone ringing off the hook with people calling in to say they'd spotted those hoodlums running from the fire that was set in the woods. I was surprised they didn't know about our little adventure with the tanker captain.

Revelation 20:10 (ESV) ... "and the devil who had deceived them was thrown into the lake of fire and sulfur where the beast and the false prophet were, and they will be tormented day and night forever and ever."

As I was about to hold out my hands for the handcuffs, Billy piped up and said, "What are you talking about, officer? We've been here since before the movie started. We wanted to get a good spot." The policeman just raised an eyebrow and grunted for us to turn around. "Put your hands behind your backs." he ordered sternly, and just like that, we were in handcuffs.

Billy started begging. "Please let us go! We won't sneak in here anymore. I promise. Please?"

Unfortunately, the good officer was having none of our promises. He said, "You boys are going to jail for a long time!" They walked us to the back of the drive-in lot and stuffed us into an unmarked police car, joking about how we would be taken advantage of from men in the city jail.

In the back of the police car, I asked Billy what would happen to us. Billy said he was more worried about what Dad would do to us than he was about what the police would do.

Isaiah 54:2 (ESV) … "Enlarge the place of your tent, and let the curtains of your habitations be stretched out; do not hold back; lengthen your cords and strengthen your stakes."

The remainder of the ten-minute ride was very quiet as we pondered our fate. I imagined myself, old and gray, walking out from between the huge iron gates of the federal prison. To our surprise, instead of the police station, they took us to Ferry Point Park, a dark and deserted place underneath the Whitestone Bridge at the spot where the Bronx and Queens connect.

If you are not familiar with the geography of New York, here's a quick lesson for you. There are five boroughs: The Bronx, Queens, Manhattan, Brooklyn, and Staten Island. The Bronx is the only borough that requires saying, "The" before the name.

Since we lived in the Bronx, I always imagined that the formality of its name gave it more respect. It was kind of like saying "Mister" before someone's name. The Bronx is the only borough connected to the rest of New York State, and although most people think of New York State and New York City as one and the same, the state of New York is, in fact, very large and very rural in some areas. We never got the chance to see that part of New York, but we somehow felt more connected to our state by virtue of our geography.

Romans 8:18 (ESV) ... "For I consider that the sufferings of this present time are not worth comparing with the glory that is to be revealed to us."

Now back to Ferry Point Park! It was dark and late when we rolled into the parking lot. One by one, we got out of the car, and the police officer took off our handcuffs. That's when the slapping started. A smack to the head for one, a kick in the butt for another, a punch to the chest for the third as the police officers told us they were letting us go. (This was well before any of the citizenry was hollering about police brutality!) The clincher was that we had to walk all the way home.

They gave us a good talking to about our future, and what would become of us if we didn't straighten up and fly right. Finally, they climbed into their car and drove off. We stood like statues, absorbing the reality of our situation, and then burst out laughing, rubbing our heads and groaning over our injuries at the same time.

I don't know how I ever made it home that night with the trauma my body had endured during our big day of adventure. When we got home, we found Dad drunk, fast asleep on the couch. Thankfully, we were able to avoid a belt-lashing, and we tip-toed off to bed. All was right with the world!

WHAT'S A FISTFIGHT
BETWEEN FRIENDS?

▲ ▲ ▲

JAMES 4:1 (NIV) … "WHAT causes fights and quarrels among you? Don't they come from your desires that battle within you?"

While growing up in the Bronx in those years, fighting between friends was as common as finding a garden snake. By now, I was hanging out with two boys named Louie and Frankie in school. Both boys were baby Italian wise guys. Louie was older than Frankie and me.

Louie had been "left back" in school a few times, and was in the habit of being an instigator. In fact, he really enjoyed instigating fights between Frankie and me. After school, the three of us would shoot hoops in the park behind the twenty story building. Louie was the very athletic type, and he would challenge us to beat him, two against one. He could beat us fairly easily, although every once in a while, Frankie and I would win a game. Sometimes, I played Frankie one on one, and those were good games, very physical, but challenging. Most of the time Frankie and I would end up in a pile on the court, fighting and punching the daylights out of each other, while Louie stood there laughing.

I liked Louie because he was very good at math, and he would let me cheat off him whenever we took a test. Frankie was a good artist, and he taught me to draw, which I came to enjoy.

Kenneth was in our class, and he was also a good artist. Frankie and I would compete with him, trying to "outdraw" him in a contest. We all drew to the best of our abilities, while Louie would try to start an argument or fight between us over our art competitions.

John 6:2 (NIV) ... "and a great crowd of people followed him because they saw the signs he had performed by healing the sick."

We had a gentle giant in our class named Charlie. I don't know how he did it, but Louie managed to get a fight going between Charley and me. The fight was scheduled for after school, and by the time the last bell rang, everyone in the school knew about the impending fistfight.

After school fights were fairly common. Boys still settled their differences in the schoolyard after the 3:00 bell. Walking out the door, Louie kept filling my eardrum, like a corner coach in a boxing ring, telling me I could whip Charlie. Frankie was right there with him instigating the fight.

By the time I made it out to the schoolyard, I had convinced myself that I would kick Charlie's rear end. But Charlie didn't want to fight. He was a big, quiet guy with no axe to grind with the likes of me, and he seemed nervous about the fight. We walked up the block, away from the school, so we wouldn't get into trouble with the teachers.

About thirty kids followed us, hooting and hollering about the fight they were about to see and betting on the outcome. We dropped our books and just stood there with our fists tightly clenched, staring at each other, each waiting for the other to throw the first punch.

I don't remember who started it, but suddenly the fight was in full swing.

Psalm 107:28 (NIV) ... "Then they cried to the LORD in their trouble, and he delivered them from their distress."

Within moments, I was cursing myself for leaving the schoolyard. I wanted nothing more than to have a teacher show up to stop the bloodbath! The scenario I saw in my mind was exactly the opposite of what I had envisioned. Charlie was kicking my rear end! I got a few good shots in during one exchange, but he now had me on the ground, and he was just pounding on me. I couldn't see how to get out from under him, and I knew I was bleeding. I felt like I was going to pass out. Out of nowhere, someone jumped out of the crowd of cheering onlookers and grabbed me. Before I knew it, I was in a Volkswagen Beetle, racing away from Charlie and the screaming crowd.

The Volkswagen Beetle was a very popular car in the 1960s, but I only knew one person who had one—Kevin's brother Patty. Kevin, whose Mom was hit at the bus stop, had two older half-brothers, Patty and Billy. They had a different father than Kevin, which was really confusing to me. He also had two full sisters because they shared the same mother and father.

The "half" and "full" was hard for me to understand because no one else we knew had a family with kids from different fathers. I wasn't sure how that worked exactly, but I tried my best to keep it straight. As Patty was driving me back to the projects, I blubbered "Thanks" and tried to explain how things had gotten out of control.

He just smiled and said, "You were the one winning the fight! I just wanted to stop you from hurting the other guy."

I just laughed, knowing he was only trying to put a smile on my face. As I climbed out of the car, Patty handed me a dollar and told me he bet on the other kid and lost. He also gave me a "stay-out-of-trouble" speech.

Just thinking about going back to school the next day was a nightmare. I thought about how embarrassed I was going to feel and how all the guys would harass me for chickening out of the fight. I forced myself to get up and dress for school the next day, dreading the abuse I would take when I saw my classmates. I felt as if I were dreaming when I walked into the school the next morning and was greeted with cheers and congratulations—as if I had won the fight with Charlie.

Isaiah 52:8 (CEV) … "Everyone on guard duty, sing and celebrate! Look! You can see the Lord *returning to Zion."*

Unbeknownst to me, Charlie really was a tough guy, and no one had ever beaten him before. No one had even wanted to fight him, and apparently everyone knew that except me. Charlie even shook my hand and said, "It was a good fight." I got slapped on the back and congratulated all day simply for being brave enough to take on Charlie in a fight. Suddenly, my chest was puffed out, and I walked with my chin in the air, like a lion after a kill. I felt like "King of the World," though secretly I was happy to have escaped with my life!

Louie's friend Phil was the captain of the crossing guards, a group called the "AAA." They all had really cool-looking badges that resembled real police badges. "Do you and Frankie want to join the force?" Louie asked. However, we knew we couldn't become guards because that was an honor bestowed only on select kids who were in a special "IGC" class—"Individual Gifted Children." I was sure I didn't qualify.

Louie said, "I could pull a few strings and get you onto the force."

Sure enough, two days later, there we were the "Three Musketeers", standing on the corner with our badges shining in the sun. One of the great things about being a guard in the AAA was that you would get out of class a full ten minutes early!

Louie got himself into the force as a sergeant, and Frankie and I were privates—the lowest of the low. We each had a "post"—an assigned corner where we stood to help walk the younger crowd across the street. When it was time for us to start our tour of duty, Captain Phil would stretch his neck out like a rooster and crow, "On post!" Everyone would scurry to his corner. When it was time to leave, Phil would crow again, "Off post!" and we would disband.

Acts 8:33 (NIV) ... "In his humiliation he was deprived of justice. Who can speak of his descendants? For his life was taken from the earth."

In the winter, when it was all of 2° outside, I was assigned the post with no shelter or windbreak. Some corner posts had bushes and trees to hide behind in an effort to keep warm. My post had absolutely nothing to block the wind.

Louie always got a post inside the building with Phil during the winter. On our lunch break, while we were "off post" one day, we walked to the school lobby to get in out of the cold. The snow was up to our ankles that day, and we felt like popsicles.

We stopped to have a snowball fight, and a teacher appeared out of nowhere. I was caught red-handed, holding a snowball in my fist.

The teacher asked, "What are you doing?"

The dumbest answer came to my mind as I said, "Licking the snowball because I'm thirsty."

The teacher didn't believe me. She said, "You were going to throw the snowball at the kids going into the school." She even dared me to throw it—as if I would be slightly insane enough to do it right there in front of a teacher! I couldn't believe my ears. The teacher was actually telling me to throw the snowball.

So I did as dared. I just went ahead and flung the snowball right at Frankie's head. At that point, the teacher grabbed me by the arm and dragged me into the building.

After lunch, all of the students lined up in the gymnasium while the principal croaked into his microphone about the afternoon activities. In the midst of the festivities, I was dragged into the gymnasium, right up to the principal, with the entire student population watching in anticipation.

The teacher whispered in the principal's ear, telling him about my transgression with the snowball. The Principal, who was still holding the microphone and staring at me in disbelief, yelled, "Fire him!" His words rang loud and clear throughout the gymnasium, bouncing off the cement walls with deafening force.

I was mortified! I took off into the hallway, sobbing and shaking like a baby. I couldn't catch my breath. I was so hysterical. I had just been humiliated in front of all of my friends and in front of the entire student body. My teacher found me and took me aside, trying to calm me down.

Galatians 6:1 (ESV) … "Brothers, if anyone is caught in any transgression, you who are spiritual should restore him in a spirit of gentleness. Keep watch on yourself, lest you too be tempted."

It took about ten minutes before I could talk. Even my father had never shook me up like that. I was angry because the teacher had set me up, challenging me to throw the snowball, yet never expecting me to do so.

I explained how the other teacher had dared me, even mocked me into throwing it. I said, "I believed he seriously wanted me to throw the snowball. I didn't think the teacher was kidding."

Strangely enough, my teacher seemed to understand my logic! Everyone was headed back to class now, and I could see the smirks and giggles as the line of students passed me, staring as if I was from another planet. The principal was walking down the hall toward us, looking like a stern military sergeant. My heart now raced faster than before.

My teacher told me to stay where I was, and he walked toward the principal, pulled him aside, and explained what had happened. I watched a lot of head bobbing and whispering, and I tried to figure out what they were saying.

When the whispering ended, my teacher came back to say that I was reinstated. "You can go back to your position as a guard!"

Being an "AAA" guard may have been a stupid assignment to some people, but to me, it was a great honor, and I felt vindicated to have my position back. As I walked back to my classroom overjoyed and content, I silently vowed to do the best job I could to make my teacher proud.

In spite of my silent vow, I was already plotting to get the teacher who had dared me to throw the snowball. I sat in class that afternoon, painting a mental image of a bull's eye on that teacher's head, wondering how I might get my revenge.

PETER'S UNTIMELY END

▲ ▲ ▲

Job 6:8 (BBE) … "If only I might have an answer to my prayer, and God would give me my desire!"

Peter, and his family lived in our building, and they were one of my customers on my paper route. On this particular day, I had been knocking on doors to make my collections. When I got to Peter's apartment, Peter answered my knock. Though we knew each other well, we didn't often hang out together. Peter had a younger brother, Billy, and he was about the same age as my younger brother, Jimmy.

While I was waiting for the weekly payment, Peter asked me if he could take over my paper route. He had heard that I was getting tired of the route and that I was thinking of letting it go. I didn't think much about his request. I told him that I might be ready to hand it over in a few weeks. "I'll let you know." I wasn't really sure if I wanted to give up the money I made, though it wasn't all that much cash.

Still the route was an easy one, and it did give me some spending money. We agreed that I would get back to him after I made my decision, so I said goodbye and went on my way. I had no idea that this encounter would be our last, I would never again see Peter alive.

2 Corinthians 12:9 (ESV) … "But he said to me, 'My grace is sufficient for you, for my power is made perfect in weakness.' Therefore I will boast all the more gladly of my weaknesses, so that the power of Christ may rest upon me."

The very next day, I was walking home from school, minding my own business, and as I approached the building, I saw a number of people standing around, as if they weren't sure what to do or where to go. I knew with that intuition or sixth sense that we sometimes get that there was something very wrong. The very air around the building seemed constricted, as if each brick held its breath in anticipation. People were standing in small knots and groups, whispering and shaking their heads.

I wanted to know what was happening, and I wanted to know right then. I couldn't stand the suspense any longer! Yet, a part of me was sure that I didn't want to know at all.

When I saw the ambulance and police car parked in front of our building, I knew it must be bad. It must be really bad! And it was! Peter was dead; he had hung himself.

There were whispered questions and insinuations about whether he had done it on purpose, but no one ever knew for sure. I preferred to think it was just a dumb accident, though that didn't make me feel much better about the whole thing.

Peter, who was my age with whom I had talked only yesterday, was dead. How could that be? Shouldn't I have somehow known that something bad was coming? Should I have felt it?

On the day he died, Peter had stayed home from school because he was sick. From what the police could determine, he was practicing his Boy Scout knots with a rope, and he made a loop and put it over his head, then tied it to a pole across from the kitchen door. From there, the picture was gray. Seemingly he had stood on a chair and either slipped or jumped. No one knew for sure. How could we?

His younger brother, Billy, was in school at the time, right across the street at St. John's. From his classroom window, Billy could see his family's apartment. Billy later said, "I kept looking out of the classroom window at our apartment across the street. I had an eerie feeling that something was wrong."

Habakkuk 1:13 (NIV) ... "Your eyes are too pure to look on evil; you cannot tolerate wrongdoing. Why then do you tolerate the treacherous? Why are you silent while the wicked swallow up those more righteous than themselves?"

After school, Billy ran home and anxiously pushed open his apartment door. The chain lock was on, so he couldn't get the door open more than a few inches. "Peter," he called, "open the door!" There was no response. When he peered through the crack in the kitchen door, he could see Peter hanging from the rope, his body limp and lifeless.

Billy was terrified. He started to scream and bang on the door, and the neighbors, hearing the commotion, came out and tried in vain to break the chain from the outside so they could get into the apartment. When they finally got in, it was too late. Peter was already dead when they cut him down.

I remember the story Billy told and how impossible it seemed that Peter no longer would answer my knock, and that none of us would ever see him again. The situation was unfathomable to me, and worse was the question that lurked in everyone's mind. "Did he do it on purpose, and if so, what would cause a boy so young to take his own life?"

The fact that we would never have the answer to that terrible question made the death seem even more mysterious and terrible. I couldn't get it out of my head.

Ephesians 5:4 (NIV) ... "*Nor should there be obscenity, foolish talk or coarse joking, which are out of place, but rather thanksgiving.*"

At the dinner table, we talked about what had happened to Peter, and Dad lectured us, telling us never to put a rope around our head or neck. During one such discussion, my brother, Tommy, said something that I would never forget. Perhaps it was the awful way Peter died. Perhaps it was the mystery of the cause and meaning of his death. I don't know, but I thought what Tommy said that day was the cruelest, most vicious statement I had ever heard. I was very appalled at my own guilty chuckle as I stifled it behind an upraised hand.

Peter's mom was a very nice lady whom I liked very much. Whenever I collected for my paper route, she always gave me a big tip. I thought she was great, and I knew I could count on her every week for that generous gesture. The picture of that sweet woman crying over her son's tragic death made what Tommy said nearly impossible to believe.

It seems that a few of Tommy's friends had telephoned Peter's family in the hours shortly after Peter's body was found and taken away—even before the family could come to grips with his death. When the family answered the phone, the boys said, "Tell Peter he can't HANG OUT with us anymore!" The boys then laughed and hung up.

Peter's mom practically had a nervous breakdown when she heard that message, and her husband went berserk.

*Proverbs 3:5 (ESV) ... "Trust in the L*ORD* with all your heart, and do not lean on your own understanding."*

Peter's family moved from the projects not too long after that incident, and while I could fully understand why they would not want to stay in that apartment, I found their absence even more disturbing. It was a constant reminder of what had happened in that apartment.

For a long time, I harbored a secret guilt about that day. I kept thinking about the conversation I had with Peter about my paper route. What if I had told Peter that he could have the route? What if he had to deliver papers that day in the building? He might have been with me, learning the route, running up and down the stairs, laughing together and having a great time. If I had done it differently, maybe he would still be alive today.

I never told anyone about that conversation or about the guilt I felt over his death. It took a long time for me to get over that! It occurs to me that most of the things I have learned in life stem from those early years of my childhood—the people I met, the places I went, and the things I saw and experienced.

School didn't teach me much about life. Yes, I learned to read, write, and add numbers. But I learned most of what I know about life from the bumps, bruises, disappointments, shocks, and hurts of my early years. In the outside world, I learned that death wasn't something to be afraid of. Nothing compared to the lessons learned on the streets of the Bronx with my friends at my side.

CAT TOSSING AND SPITBALLS

▲ ▲ ▲

John 1:5 (NIV) ... "The light shines in the darkness, and the darkness has not overcome it."

I cannot say I remember much about what happened in school, but I do remember those unforgettable moments like the New York City blackout of 1965. The entire East Coast was plunged into darkness, and with it, our projects and my apartment. Like a leaf floating help-lessly downstream, we endured the blackout with the other families, and though I never thought much about electricity until then, on that day, I realized how important it really was to our everyday lives. Seemingly, we could do nothing that didn't require power.

Nevertheless, being us, we managed to agitate anyway! We ran up and down the hallways, spooking people in the dark. Outside, the world seemed to have ground to a halt. There were no sounds of radio or television drifting out of open windows, no traffic lights, and no street lights. An eerie silence seemed to have fallen over the city. People were trapped in elevators, and we watched the police and firemen running up and down the street, going to rescue them.

In the course of these events, the rescue teams came into our building too, and my brother Billy paid rapt attention to their activities. I didn't quite know why at the time, but by the next day when the lights came back on, Billy seemed to have learned an awful lot about elevators and electricity. As usual, I knew he was up to no good!

He had figured out how we could run the elevator with the door open, watching from the lobby as the elevator rocketed upward, growing smaller as it drew up and away. It seemed that all he needed to pull off this miracle was a comb and a piece of aluminum foil from an empty cigarette pack. Gumby, Billy and I were standing in the lobby about to venture into this vast new territory of troublemaking. Billy walked over to the elevator, examined the door for a moment, and then fit a comb wrapped in foil into the opening to access the door lock. He had discovered that if you put the comb and foil into the slot, it would trigger the elevator, and it would take off for the upper floors.

James 3:15 (NIV) ... "Such 'wisdom' does not come down from heaven but is earthly, unspiritual, demonic."

From our vantage point in the lobby, we could stand there and watch the elevator speed away, and what a thrill that was! It was almost as thrilling as getting on top of the elevator. Billy had figured out how to do that too!

If you pressed the emergency button from inside the elevator, stopping the elevator between floors, a skinny kid—like one of us, for instance—could reach an arm up to the next level and push a lever to open the door. So if we stopped the elevator between the fifth and sixth floor and then pushed the sixth floor elevator lever, the door would open and voilà! We could crawl right out of the elevator and stand on the sixth floor, looking at the top half of the elevator floating before us in the shaft. Sure enough, we had our access to the top of the elevator!

Once we got this routine down pat, we would ride the top of the elevators for hours, listening in on conversations and making weird noises that would freak out those inside the elevator. The first time I rode the top of the elevator, we headed up to the twelfth floor. "Billy, what happens when we get to the top floor?"

Of course, he said, "We'll be crushed to death."

Still in my gullible phase, I believed every word Billy told me, and I silently prayed for my life as we approached the top of the elevator shaft. You've probably already figured out that we didn't get crushed to death on the twelfth floor.

When we got to the top, Billy and Gumby said we were getting off. We jumped off the elevator roof and onto a platform with a door. This door opened into a small room where the custodians and police visited at different times of the day. The real purpose of the room was for emergencies, and qualified authorities used it to get to the elevators quickly. In this room was another door that led to the iron staircase.

1 Kings 6:8 (NASB) ... "The doorway for the lowest side chamber was on the right side of the house; and they would go up by winding stairs to the middle story, and from the middle to the third."

All twelve-story buildings in the projects had the same stairway structure with three different sets of stairs, and each one connected to one of the wings of our building. Two of the stairways were cement from the first floor all the way up to the twelfth floor. The third staircase was made of iron. Standing on the twelfth floor of the iron staircase, you could look all the way down to the first floor, and it was a dizzying height.

Like the good soldiers we were, we felt it our duty to make trouble wherever we could. This place and time was no exception. We would stand on the landing of the twelfth-floor iron staircase and try to aim our spitballs so that they would land on the hands of the people using the staircase below. As they held the iron railing, their hands would protrude slightly out from the skeleton of the staircase, and they made great targets for our fine aim. If you got lucky, the person below would look up at you, and you might even be able to spit right in the person's eye!

When we did get lucky and landed the treasured "eye shot," the victim would come racing up the stairs from three or four floors below, cursing and promising to do physical harm to us when they caught us. We would bolt out of the staircase, and depending on which floor we were lurking on, we had plenty of options for escape. We could use either of the other two staircases, or we could go up or down the iron stairs and exit on another floor.

When the victims arrived at the floor from where we had launched our attack, they had to decide which staircase we had taken, and they had to choose from the two cement staircases, as well as the floors above or below where we originally stood. They rarely chose correctly! We could also confuse the victims by escaping via the terrace, and that escape was a daring escapade in itself.

Ezekiel 41:10 (TLB) ... "Thirty-five feet away from the terrace, on both sides of the Temple, was another row of rooms down in the inner court."

Every floor except the first floor had a terrace, which was usually kept locked. On each floor, one designated family held the key to the terrace, so we were out of luck as far as legal access. The terrace had windows, and we could jump up and crawl in through these, and we often did so when we were being chased. We would hide quietly in the corner of the terrace until the coast was clear. Our final point of emergency escape was to disappear into someone's apartment.

Many times, we would escape to Gumby's apartment on the eleventh floor, as it was the closest to our point of attack. From any terrace in the building, you could look out toward the front of the property through a gated mesh fence. The fence was in place to ensure that no one fell from the terrace.

In our continuing effort to find every way possible to make trouble, we would cut through the fence with wire clippers and use the opening to throw things from the terrace onto the unsuspecting people walking in and out of the lobby.

Acts 14:10 (ESV) … "said in a loud voice, 'Stand upright on your feet.' And he sprang up and began walking."

One day, Billy decided to throw a cat from the third-floor terrace. As we watched the cat plummeting toward the ground from the third floor, we waited with anticipation to hear the SPLAT sound that would tell us the cat had reached its final destination. To our amazement, the cat landed on all four legs and simply ran away, apparently unharmed. On that day, I decided that everything I had heard about cats having nine lives was indeed true!

Unfortunately, Gumby was with us the day of the cat tossing, and he was a cat lover. At all times, Gumby had at least two cats in his house. When we went downstairs after the cat tossing, Billy and Gumby got into a fistfight over the offense.

Billy just did not like cats. The only cat for which he had an ounce of sympathy was a Siamese cat that he once found in the street.

Proverbs 12:10 (NASB) … "A righteous man has regard for the life of his animal, But even the compassion of the wicked is cruel."

Even that Siamese cat was the victim of abuse. Billy was thinking of throwing the cat down the incinerator, but as he was holding it, he decided, in a show of kindness, to simply let the cat go with a good tail-pulling. He yanked the cat's tail hard, and it let out a wail that sounded like the siren for a fire truck.

The sound started as a low and menacing growl and then, as Billy pulled harder on the tail, the wail got louder and louder until it sounded like the siren for a three-alarm fire. Instead of having the effect the cat had probably hoped—that Billy would let it skitter off into the shadows and escape, the yowling gave Billy yet another idea.

He ran into the apartment with the struggling cat tucked under his arm and came back out with his bicycle. Once outside, he tucked the cat into a makeshift basket he had assembled in the apartment and pedaled happily around the neighborhood for the rest of the day with the cat trapped inside the basket. As he pedaled, he tugged the cat's tail to make the siren sound. It was a real sight to see, and we laughed heartily, especially since Gumby wasn't with us!

Job 29:21 (ESV) ... "Men listened to me and waited and kept silence for my counsel."

Billy didn't get away without a fight. Robbie was also a cat lover, and he had one Siamese cat living in his house. When Robbie saw Billy running the "cat siren," he got angry.

"Billy, either give me the cat or there will be a fight."

However, Billy wasn't going to give up without some negotiation. "Aw, Robbie, I just want to ride the cat around the building a few more times. Then I'll give him to you."

All ended well for the cat, in that he ended up comfortably living at Robbie's house and certainly received better treatment. Every time we went to Robbie's apartment after that, we would wait until he walked out of the room, and one of us would pull on the cat's tail just to hear him make the siren sound—for old time's sake, of course!

Robbie would run back into the room and glare at us, trying to find the culprit. We would all fold our hands in our laps and smile. When he asked, Who pulled the cat's tail?" we would say in harmony, "Nobody!" Robbie would give us a simmering look and leave the room. Pulling the cat's tail was one of our favorite pranks!

Matthew 10:29 (ESV) ... "Are not two sparrows sold for a penny? And not one of them will fall to the ground apart from your Father."

One day we were walking in through the back of our building, joking around and poking fun at one another as usual. Gumby happened to look up at his eleventh-floor apartment window and noticed his cat playing at his bedroom window. The window and the curtains were both open. We followed Gumby's gaze to see what he was looking at, and just as we all looked up, the cat fell out of the window. That cat's legs were flailing as he fell, and his mouth was wide open in what was no doubt a silent version of the cat siren.

Based on our previous experience with cats having nine lives, we just naturally assumed this cat would survive the fall, and Billy and I were laughing as we watched him tumble toward the ground. Gumby was furious with us, and panic was written all over his face! After what seemed like an eternity, the cat hit the ground, and we could hear the loud "thump." We ran quickly over to see how he was doing, knowing all too well when he did not get up and run away. The cat was still breathing, but his eyes and mouth didn't look so well.

Gumby cried all the way into the building and up the elevator, as we silently carried the cat upstairs to his apartment. The cat lived for a few hours then died.

Consequently, I had to modify my firm belief that all cats had nine lives. I now knew that not every cat was quite so blessed!

THE WORLD INTRUDES

▲ ▲ ▲

I Samuel 8:6 (NIV) ... "But when they said, 'Give us a king to lead us,' this displeased Samuel; so he prayed to the Lord."

When I look back on those early years now, I realize that for children back-then or maybe at any time in history, it is often as if the outside world does not exist. Our world was never any bigger than the projects and within a few mile radius. Most of the time, it was limited to our building and the surrounding lots.

In the seclusion of our apartment dinner was always at 5:00 p.m. We had to make sure we made it home by then, or we would be confined in our rooms after dinner. A fate worse than death! During dinner, the 5:00 news was normally blasting from the television, so we did know some of what was happening in the outside world—though we weren't always sure we understood it. Once dinner started Dad ruled as the king, and when he said you to do something, you just did it, no questions asked.

Genesis 9:4 (NIV) ... "But you must not eat meat that has its lifeblood still in it."

One day at dinner, Tommy foolishly said he didn't like the mashed potatoes Dad had made. Since Mom was in the hospital most of the time, Dad did the cooking in those days. He wasn't so bad at the domestic routine.

Dad told Tommy that he expected him to eat his potatoes. Furthermore, if Tommy didn't eat his potatoes, Dad said he would see to it that Tommy wore those potatoes on his head.

His tone left no doubt in my mind that he was serious! A few minutes went by, and Tommy had not touched the suspect spuds, so Dad simply stood up, walked over to Tommy's chair, picked up his plate, and dumped it over his head—potatoes and all.

The rest of us started eating our potatoes faster than ever, cramming forks full in our mouths until there was no more room. We looked like a family of chipmunks packing away their winter food. Through chomping cheeks, we each commented on how good the potatoes were. We had to admit, we'd never tasted anything else like them!

Proverbs 15:17 (NIV) ... "Better a small serving of vegetables with love than a fattened calf with hatred."

As Tommy was cleaning up the leftover mess that had been his dinner, Dad reminded us never to doubt his word. Dad would often make a beef stew for dinner that Billy and I hated. Tommy loved Dad's beef stew. He thought it was the greatest meal in the world. Billy and I would try to gag it down and end up sick to our stomachs, while Dad and his buddy, Tommy, would laugh and gobble it down, proclaiming the virtues of beef stew.

Billy's mind was always working, and he eventually came up with a great idea regarding Dad's beef stew. He would spread his napkin on his lap, put the stew on his spoon and then drop it into the napkin when Dad wasn't looking. This ingenious method seemed to work fine for Billy, so I thought I would try it. Of course I got caught!

I wasn't about to take the blame alone, so I snitched on Billy and told Dad it was Billy's idea. The beef stew landed over Billy's head as I gobbled mine down as fast as I could trying not to laugh as I watched the tears come pouring down Billy's cheeks.

Luke 21:8 (NASB) ... "And He said, 'See to it that you are not misled; for many will come in My name, saying, 'I am He,' and, 'The time is near.' Do not go after them."

As for the outside world—it kept turning! The "British Invasion" was making history as the English music of the 60s floated across the "pond" and invaded our country. With its roots firmly planted in the blues and old American Rock 'n' Roll, the new English sound swept the U.S. We seemed to learn much about yellow submarines, eight days in a week, fools on a hill, a hard day's night, while others taught us about satisfaction, getting off someone's cloud, and painting stuff black. At the same time, Motown was teaching us that clown's cry, we need to get ready, we have to stop in the name of love, our ABC's, it's the same old song, how we were uptight and everything was about r-e-s-p-e-c-t.

My G.I Joe action figures were derived from actual events going on a world away as I would often see pictures on the news of anti-war demonstrators, or "hippies," as most people called them. None of this made a lot of sense to me, and I had no clue to the differing opinions and rhetoric I heard booming from microphones and bullhorns.

Rosa Parks became the poster woman for the anti-segregation movement as she held tight to her seat and refused to give it up to a white man. All kinds of protesting was going on in the black community. Back then, African-Americans were referred to as "colored."

Romans 13:1 (NASB) ... "Every person is to be in subjection to the governing authorities For there is no authority except from God, and those which exist are established by God."

We watched the flickering images on our fuzzy screens and twisted the antenna for better reception, but we never got a full picture of what was happening across the country. We were, after all, just kids!

Dr. Martin Luther King's name was on television a great deal. My mind envisioned an invisible line somewhere separating people. I heard the words "Democrats" and "Republicans" through echoes of anger. At that point, I would just climb back into my four-block paradise.

Grownups played games, and one was with the Russians and how fast we could get to the moon. The winner would have extreme bragging rights. As our country was exploring space, I was exploring my neighborhood and the surrounding areas without fear of the unknown.

Exodus 23:7 (NASB) ... "Keep far from a false charge, and do not kill the innocent or the righteous, for I will not acquit the guilty."

Space seemed pretty simple to me, but then I didn't understand the scope and the impact of the space program. To me, the moon was nothing more than a great backdrop for a cold Halloween night, and my explorations were much more exciting than any space mission.

I remember knowing by the reactions of the adults in my life, that certain things were serious. Still, I was much more interested in the music and televisions shows of the time. They were great, to say the least. Every couple of weeks throughout the decade of the 1960s, someone would come along and knock the Beatles off the number-one spot on the music charts. They always bounced back, and the Beatles would be at the top of the charts for years.

There was only one real radio station for the music of that age in New York City and the surrounding boroughs, and that was 77 WABC! One super star radio Deejay was "Cousin Brucie." Whenever he shouted out his name, I believed he was actually a family cousin. It took years, and with disappointment, for me to figure out that we were not related.

In our apartment, the radio was always set to that station, and as the children in the family all came of age, the radio seemed to be on all the time. We were growing up learning about the world. Yet, the television shows we watched were still a haven for the innocence we fought so hard to keep.

Ephesians 2:2, 3 (ESV) ... "In which you once walked, following the course of this world, following the prince of the power of the air, the spirit that is now at work in the sons of disobedience—among whom we all once lived in the passions of our flesh, carrying out the desires of the body and the mind, and were by nature children of wrath, like the rest of mankind."

As our nation lost and mourned numerous leaders and watched a war we could not understand, we huddled in our living rooms and looked to our favorite shows to take us away from the unimaginable. Some thoughts flowing into my mind from the shows were that if you twitched your nose just right, you could make things appear and disappear. I could slide down a pole, and my clothes would change, blasting me from a secret cave. I could fly and have superhuman strength. Horses could talk, and if you rode a horse and wore a white hat, you were a good guy. Short stories from "The Twilight Zone" and "The Outer Limits" would scare the daylights out of me. I could go where no man has gone before, every deserted island had bottles with "Jeannies" in them, I could adventure to the bottom of the ocean in a submarine, and "Green Acres" was the place to be.

I wanted to be a sheriff in "Dodge City." If I sneezed just right I could be a hero in the Army. With twin girls, one is always good and the other bad. I would rather be the sidekick and know martial arts than be the heroic hero himself.

Cable and "Pay TV" were distant dreams, and the era of the remote was not a button to push but a child to order. The only television channels we had were local network channels: CBS (channel 2), NBC (channel 4), ABC (channel 7), and the original independent Fox channel. The syndicated stations like WOR 9, and WPIX (channel 11) were a distant second to the big three networks and the upstart Fox 5. And PBS (channel 13) carried mysteriously boring "public television" that didn't interest us.

Matthew 24:22 (ESV) … "And if those days had not been cut short, no human being would be saved. But for the sake of the elect those days will be cut short."

There was always a network movie on at 9:00 p.m. If you watched a good movie the night before, you were assured that your friends saw the same one. It was really the only thing on television, so we would always talk about it in great detail the day after it aired.

One night as I woke up for a bathroom break, Tommy was watching the 11:00 p.m. late news. The screen was alight with pictures of exploding bombs. I asked Tommy what was going on, and he answered, "The Russians set off nuclear bombs. The news anchorman announced they were headed toward the U.S.—unless our Air Force bombers can shoot them down first. If they can't, we'll all be dead by morning."

Tommy seemed genuinely concerned, so of course, I was concerned too. I didn't know why the Russians would want to kill all of us, but I certainly didn't want to be blown out of my bed in the middle of the night. I couldn't sleep all night because we lived in the LaGuardia Airport flight path, and every time a plane flew overhead, I thought it was the Russians coming to blow me to smithereens.

The next morning lying in bed as my eyes opened, I had a feeling of joy that I was still alive.

ABRAHAM, MARTIN AND JOHN

▲ ▲ ▲

DEUTERONOMY 27:25 (NIV) "'CURSED be anyone who takes a bribe to shed innocent blood.' And all the people shall say, 'Amen.'"

I remember the day when Dr. Martin Luther King, Jr., was assassinated. Television images of burning buildings and riots were fascinating to watch, and just one of the many television reports of the time that I watched without a full grasp that it wasn't just television.

Robert Kennedy was killed shortly thereafter. The murders of John and Robert Kennedy and Dr. King will stay with me for the rest of my life as events that silenced and stymied even the grownups in my life. By their reactions I understood exactly how important these people were and the profound change that had taken place in our world. I didn't, at the time, understand why they were important. I felt they must all have been good people for the adults in our country to react as they did.

Sometime later, the lead singer of a popular group named "Dion and the Belmonts" recorded a solo single. Dion Dimucci was also from the Bronx, and he had hit songs like "The Wanderer" and "Teenager in Love." But in my eyes, his blockbuster song was "Abraham, Martin and John," which addressed the assassinations of

Abraham Lincoln, Martin Luther King, Jr., John F. Kennedy and Robert Kennedy.

Following the death of the two Kennedy brothers and Dr. King, Dimucci sang this moving song about the exceptional character of these men. Even hearing the song today stirs up tears and emotions. When I first heard the song, I recall feeling a strange sense of loss—as if I had actually known these men that died. I still feel that way today!

As I came of age, and my childhood was coming to an end, my only real passion was still having fun with my friends. Yet, every now and then, I would poke my head out into the outside world to get a peek and a glimpse of what was going on there.

Proverbs 23:21 (ESV) ... "for the drunkard and the glutton will come to poverty, and slumber will clothe them with rags."

Maybe it was my burgeoning maturity and the growing awareness that there was indeed a world beyond my four walls. Maybe it was the fact that the world seemed to be pushing in more and more every day news of space missions, assassinations, new music and the ongoing war and protests. I felt as if I was being pulled, inextricably, into the eye of a swirling tornado, and I wanted nothing more than to be a child for a little while longer.

Every year the Castle Hill community Center had a parade that would start at the train station, work its way to the projects, ending at the Castle Hill Little League field. A circus would always follow the parade, and we looked forward to the event every year.

One particular year, the master of ceremonies was none other than our channel 7 local weatherman, Tex Antoine, a dark, suave-looking guy with a sense of humor. He would always tell some kind of joke during the course of his weather forecast, and everyone loved to watch him.

I was really excited because I had never seen a celebrity in person. Tex was on television, and he therefore qualified as a pretty big celebrity in my mind. This would be a thrill! As Tex rode down Castle Hill Avenue in the parade, he was sitting in an open convertible, and the driver was traversing the parade path very slowly, so everyone could get a good look at Tex.

Unfortunately, for me, the thrill didn't last very long. As he passed through the streets down the parade route, it became obvious that he was very drunk. Word spread through the crowd, and there were whispers and heads shaking in disgust as rumor of his nasty behavior spread among the onlookers. I was disappointed though I understood from personal experience that people like Tex always seemed to end up alone and sad and miserable.

Matthew 12:36 (ESV) … "I tell you, on the day of judgment people will give account for every careless word they speak."

We had numerous examples of Tex's kind of behavior in the projects, and it certainly wasn't foreign to me. Time and again, we would often see our own Catholic priest stumbling down the street drunk out of his mind. Although with Tex, I felt dejected and sad to know that he was just like everyone else. To top it all off, at the end of the parade, I tried to get his autograph and he told me to get lost.

Years later, my premonition was realized. Tex got himself fired from the television station by making a joke on the air about a young girl who had been brutally raped. "You know what they say about rape…" he chuckled, "There's nothing you can do about it, so just lay back and enjoy it."

We were all appalled, and his brazen comments were the talk of the projects the next day. He was summarily fired by the network and, to my knowledge, has never been on the air since. For some silly reason, I felt good about his being fired, as if he had deserved it for all the nastiness he had spread around that day at the parade.

Jude 1:19 (ESV) ... "It is these who cause divisions, worldly people, devoid of the Spirit."

Each building in the Castle Hill projects—every last one of the fourteen—had a distinct personality. You could always tell the building personality by the kids, teenagers, and grownups who lived in each building. After spending our childhood in the projects, we knew that certain buildings were home to nerds, while others housed the tough guys. Still other buildings were the residence and hangout for drunks, athletes, or the Jewish, black, Hispanic, or Irish families. I always found it curious that, no matter what building we hung out in, we were accepted.

For reasons that escape me, it wasn't the same in our building. A lot of kids wouldn't come near our building for fear of being beaten up. Brian made us aware of the Hell's Angels motorcycle club. At that time, we also became aware of gangs in the Bronx, and because Brian's older brothers were in motorcycle gangs, he would tell us stories about their adventures. Brian told us about the movie "Hells Angels on Wheels," and he said that it was playing at the drive-in movie theater, so we decided to go down there and see what this was all about.

The movie affected our attitudes and created a desire in us to become real tough guys. The song "Born to be Wild" from the movie "Easy Rider" was also an incentive to our becoming tough guys. After seeing the gangs in action on the big screen, everyone had to go out and buy a dungaree jacket, and of course, we cut off the sleeves to mimic the actors in the movie.

Deuteronomy 5:19 (ESV) "And you shall not steal."

My dad bought me one of those denim jackets because he knew how badly I wanted one, but after he saw that I had cut the sleeves off, he nearly killed me. The sneaker of choice was Converse, and I never had a pair because they were too expensive for our family to afford. I would get laughed at for wearing what we called "skips."

So when I finally got my first pair of Converse sneakers, it was like I had hit the lottery. When I wore them and my denim jacket with the cutoff sleeves, I felt like the king of the world.

We started a biker gang of our own and called ourselves "The Undertakers." Of course, we only rode bicycles! Not everyone had a bicycle, and if someone in the gang was without the necessary equipment, Billy and Matthew would take off for a few hours and come back with bikes. It was that simple! They would just take a hike up to Throggs Neck—a different part of the Bronx with mostly private homes—and go "shopping."

The kids in Throggs Neck often left their bikes outside a store when they went in to go shopping. Billy and Matthew would hop on the unguarded bikes and bring them back to the projects for the "gang" members.

Ephesians 4:28 (ESV) … "Let the thief no longer steal, but rather let him labor, doing honest work with his own hands, so that he may have something to share with anyone in need."

One day when Matthew came back from a bike heist out of breath and looking a little pale, he told us that outside the store he and Billy had seen two bikes just begging to be taken. Billy jumped on one and Matthew on the other. But the owner of the bike Matthew was stealing was coming out of the store just at that moment. He chased Matthew, who began pedaling for his life.

The owner of the bike had caught up to him! He held on to the back of the bike, yelling like of a son-of-a-gun for Matthew to stop and give him back his property. "I didn't stop though," Matthew bragged, "I turned around every few moments and smacked him in the face, trying to get him to let loose of the bike. I dragged that kid, screaming and crying for almost two blocks before he finally tripped and fell onto the concrete. Then I finally made my getaway!"

Ezekiel 38:13 (ESV) ... "Sheba and Dedan and the merchants of Tarshish and all its leaders will say to you, 'Have you come to seize spoil? Have you assembled your hosts to carry off plunder, to carry away silver and gold, to take away livestock and goods, to seize great spoil?' "

When the bikes arrived at the projects, we would take them to one of a building terraces where we would dissemble them. If a gang member needed a certain part for his bike, he could have his pick. Brian was the first to have a "chopper bike." To make this bike, Brian sawed the fork in the front of his bike in half. (The fork is the part that holds the front tire in place.) Then he sawed off another fork at the top of one of the stolen bikes and put the two forks together. When he was finished, he had a much extended front end on his bike, which was called a "chopper." He got the idea from the Hell's Angels who would do the same thing with their motorcycles.

The bike looked really cool, but I found it extremely hard to ride. Even though the other guys chopped their bikes, I decided to leave mine alone. Banana seats were a new concept in bicycle seats, and they looked pretty cool too. All of us had banana seats, and most chose to add another new accessory in bike construction, called "sissy bars." A sissy bar was a bar on the back of the banana seat that extended up along your back. I didn't go for the sissy bar on my bike because I liked to jump off my bike as it was cruising to a halt, and you couldn't do that with a sissy bar in place.

One day, I was standing in front of our building, passing the time, when I saw Jerry and Tommy T. running into the building with a bike they had stolen from one of the other buildings. They nervously ran up to the third-floor terrace where they started to disassemble the bike.

Proverbs 1:16 (ESV) ... "for their feet run to evil, and they make haste to shed blood."

About thirty minutes later, they were still taking the bike apart when a small group of kids, accompanied by the police, walked into the terrace. Tommy T. didn't wait for them to ask questions. He took off running down the stairs, while Jerry dramatically tried to tell them that he didn't steal the bike.

I thought it was rather dumb of them to steal a bike from one of the other buildings when all the kids who lived in the projects knew that we were stealing bikes from Throggs Neck. Jerry had to put the bike back together, and then the police officer took him to his apartment and told Jerry's mom what had happened.

Jerry's mom was a very petite woman, but he was scared to death of her and with good reason! She gave him a beating he wouldn't soon forget.

I went back downstairs to tell a few of the other guys what had happened, and then we all went upstairs and stood outside Jerry's front door to listen to him screaming profoundly as his mom beat the daylights out of him. We stood there laughing hysterically.

THE OLD SWIMMIN' HOLE

▲ ▲ ▲

REVELATION 22:1 (NIV) … "THEN the angel showed me the river of the water of life, as clear as crystal, flowing from the throne of God and of the Lamb."

During the hottest days of summer, we would take a swim in the East River at the very end of Castle Hill Avenue. Though we didn't have a real beach, the water served its purpose and we had a lot of fun. Everyone referred to this spot as "The End." When we asked someone where they were going, they would just say "The End," and you didn't have to ask anything more.

The best treat in the summer was to go to Orchard Beach that was up in Pelham Bay Park, about thirty minutes from the projects. The End was behind the Castle Hill Pool, and most of the families that belonged to the pool were middle class families from the projects who had enough money to join. The cost was about $85 per year, per person to join, so for a family of our size, the expense was simply too prohibitive.

Gumby's family joined the Castle Hill Pool every year, and Gumby was like a fish in the water every day, splashing around and getting brown in the sun. He developed some pretty good skills with all that swimming practice! When he entered high school, he joined the swim team, and he was a natural.

On the other hand swimming down at The End was always tricky. You had to consider the time and whether the tide was in or out.

Psalm 40:2 (NIV) … "He lifted me out of the slimy pit, out of the mud and mire; he set my feet on a rock and gave me a firm place to stand."

On a very hot day in the middle of one summer, Mom went for a swim down at The End, but the tide happened to be out when she got there. When the tide was out, it would separate the shore from the water with murky, ugly, deep mud. Unlike our biker gang, Mom didn't understand that you couldn't just walk out to get to the water when the tide was out.

Nevertheless, Mom didn't pay much attention to the conditions at hand. She simply looked toward the shimmering water and thought about how cool it would feel in the sweltering heat, and she started to walk. As she walked, she sank deeper and deeper into the mud.

Finally, I had to run all the way back to the projects to get Dad for help because Mom had gotten stuck up to her knees, and she just stood frozen in her tracks, unable to move.

Psalm 50:15 (NLT) … "Then call on me when you are in trouble, and I will rescue you, and you will give me glory."

When Dad got there, he couldn't believe what he was seeing. Mom had walked out that far and had sunk so deep into the mud— all while she was sober! He began screaming at her to just walk back to shore, and she was screaming back, "I can't!"

By this time, the tide was coming in, and if she didn't get moving soon, she would be covered in water and caught out so far away from shore that she wouldn't be able to walk back. Mom wasn't a strong swimmer, and we were all afraid she would drown.

Dad finally had to go out to the middle of the river, and taking one leg at a time, he pulled her free. With each step, he freed her feet from the muck. One step at a time, one leg at a time, all the way back to shore!

My friends and family laughed about that for quite a while, and I can still see my mom crab-walking through the mud, with my father bent over, moving from side to side to free her feet—one at a time, every time she took another step. How I wish I'd had a camera!

Romans 5:3 (ESV) ... "More than that, we rejoice in our sufferings, knowing that suffering produces endurance."

When the Scott family descended to The End, it was party time! The Scott family was just as big as ours. Mr. S. was always a treat to watch at The End because he would swim the river up and down, with even strokes—like a professional swimmer. He could swim out so far into the river that we would hardly be able to see him, and at times, I wondered if he would ever make it back to shore.

The Scott family tragedy happened when Henry, one of the Scott brothers, was riding on the Softee truck just as we did. One day, while Henry was having a jolly, good old time riding on the back of the ice cream truck heading up Castle Hill Avenue, the truck hit a bump and Henry fell off. One of his sneakers got stuck between the bumper and the truck, and he was being dragged foot first up Castle Hill Avenue. The truck dragged Henry a block or so before it stopped.

Henry almost died that day. He was listed in critical condition at Jacobi Hospital. The next days, everyone in school was talking about the accident, and our teachers asked us to send him get-well cards. Henry spent the next few months in the hospital, recovering from his injuries, and we all thought he was a real trooper.

Psalm 145:7 (NIV) … "They celebrate your abundant goodness and joyfully sing of your righteousness."

Whenever we went swimming at The End, we would make peanut butter and jelly sandwiches to take with us, and some Kool-Aid to wash down the sandwiches. Our needs were quite simple!

When the Scott family went to The End, it was a real festival. They would bring about 12 to 15 family members and close friends, and they would make a barbeque pit on the shore to cook chicken, steak, fish, hot dogs, hamburgers, sausages, and every kind of food you can imagine. A poor, starving gaggle of little white boys looking forlorn and hungry would stand watching—until Mrs. Scott could stand it no longer!

She would invite us to eat with them with a big smile, and we would not wait to be asked a second time. Boy, could we eat! All the while, Mr. Scott would be out there somewhere in the distance, stroking up and down the river. He went on to live a long and healthy life from all that swimming, and while he was staying healthy, we ate his food!

Lamentations 3:7 (CEV) … "God built a fence around me that I cannot climb over, and he chained me down."

The fence for the Castle Hill Pool ended down at "The End," and one day my brother Tommy took me with him to sneak over the fence into the pool. This was the first time I had been to the pool. We had to jump over three different fences to get in.

To quench my paranoia, I fell into a daydream imagining I was on a secret mission - a spy breaking into a nuclear plant or a secret facility in Russia. We took off our clothes in some bushes outside the pool so we could wear our bathing suits and look like we belonged there. After we hid our clothes in the bushes, we jumped over the fence. We reached the handball courts, and Tommy found some of his friends playing handball. I told Tommy I was going to walk around to see if I could find Gumby.

I saw Gumby in the pool with some other guys, and I walked over to say hello. He was surprised to see me and started chiding me with a con. "Here comes the guard, and he knows you sneaked in," he said, and I started to get nervous. I did get funny looks from the guards all day, as if they knew I didn't belong there. Still, it was a great day at the pool, and we never got caught.

When it was time to leave we walked out the front gate, with some pretty serious looks from the guards, but no action. We did have one little surprise awaiting us when we went back for our clothes. They were missing! We believed that "Dirty Mike" (one of the Scott brothers) took our clothes and threw them into the river, but we could never prove it. He never exactly admitted it either, but his snide look and the way he smiled at us gave him away.

With the exception of the little mishap with our clothes, our mission had been a success, and we would sneak into the pool a couple of times each year after that.

Ephesians 4:28 (KJV) ... "Let him that stole steal no more: but rather let him labor, working with his hands the thing which is good, that he may have to give to him that needs."

"Tim-Tam's" was the name of a restaurant across the street from the Castle Hill Pool. Behind the restaurant was a horse stable with a few horses and some ponies, as well as some chickens and roosters. Every now and then, we would walk over and try to let the horses out of the stables. We never had success because as soon as the owner saw us, he would bolt from the restaurant furiously and chase us away. When that plan failed we would walk to the parking lot next to Tim-Tam's, where the pool members parked their cars. Many of the car doors were left open, and we would rummage through them to see if anyone had left money. If they did, we'd make off with it, boasting about our heist.

The last stop for the number thirteen bus line was across from the pool. After the driver took his break, the bus would head back up Castle Hill Avenue. Most of the time we would sneak on the bus through the back door, and sometimes we'd just hang on to the back of the bus to catch a ride back up to the projects.

One day, Robbie, Matthew, Gumby and I took a walk down near the Sanitation Department to the water plant where Robbie's dad worked. Robbie said, "Some of my father's friends leave their car keys under the front mat of their cars when they go to work. They leave their doors unlocked! It would be easy to steal a car and take it for a joy ride."

We tried a few cars and, sure enough, we found one with the keys under the mat. We all hopped into the car and off we went. Robbie and Matthew knew how to drive, so they took turns. I was panicked about getting caught, and I let them know. "Aw, everything will be fine!"

So we drove around for a few hours and wound up in a place called Clason Point. By now, I was somewhat more relaxed, so I said, "Hey, Robbie, pull over somewhere so I can drive."

Robbie found a deserted area, and let me hop in the front seat to try my driving skills.

*I Samuel 16:17 (NIV) … "But the L*ORD *said to Samuel, 'Do not consider his appearance or his height, for I have rejected him. The L*ORD *does not look at the things people look at. People look at the outward appearance, but the L*ORD *looks at the heart.' "*

I could hardly see over the steering wheel as I stepped on the gas, slammed on the brake, then back onto the gas, jerking and bumping the car along with the two of them screaming at me. The only thing their yelling accomplished was to make me nervous, and I continued to alternate between the gas and the brakes, driving all over the road and jerking the car back and forth.

Matthew finally jumped on me, slammed his foot on the brake, and we skidded to a sudden stop. Everyone gasped as we looked up out of the windshield and discovered that Matthew had stopped the car just short of a light pole that now stood mere inches from the car's front bumper. They swore I would never drive with them again.

Robbie took over the wheel and drove about a block before the car stalled. We couldn't get it running again, and it was a 30-minute walk from Clason Point back to the projects. So we started the hike. All the way home, I got teased about my driving skills. I decided that Clason Point was not a lucky place for me because another incident would take place there.

Philippians 2:14 (NLT) … "Do everything without complaining or arguing."

We were riding our bikes in Clason Point, but I didn't have a bike at the time, so I was riding on the handlebars of Jerry's bike. My brother, Tommy, was with us, along with Tommy T., Gumby, Brian, Billy, and a few others. While crossing one of the major intersections with me on the handlebars of Jerry's bike, we had an accident! Jerry rode his bike, broadside, into a moving car. I went flying off the bike and over the car's front hood while Jerry smashed full force right into the side of the car. As unbelievable as it was, Jerry and I only had minor bumps and bruises. His bike, sadly enough, resembled a pretzel.

We all helped to carry Jerry's bike back to the projects, and on the way home, Jerry wouldn't shut up about how he was going to get into a lot of trouble for destroying his bike. My brother, Tommy, was carrying the bike, and he got fed up with listening to Jerry after a while, so he threw the bike into the street and yelled, "Carry it yourself, Jerry! And none of the rest of you are to help him!"

Jerry started to cry and begged for help in carrying the bike. We just kept walking, ignoring his pleas with Jerry's cries for help slowly fading behind us.

About one hour later, we were standing in front of our building, when we saw Jerry, still crying and struggling up the hill with his bike. We stood laughing and watching as he made his way to the building. None of us moved to help him.

Jerry did get in a bundle of trouble for destroying his bike. I have to admit, I felt relieved to be alive and relatively unharmed, and I hoped he did too. We had really dodged a bullet by coming out of the accident in one piece, and I thought that was a lot more important than his stupid bike!

THE "FRESH-AIR-FUND" KID

▲ ▲ ▲

DEUTERONOMY 15:11 (ESV) … "FOR there will never cease to be poor in the land. Therefore I command you, 'You shall open wide your hand to your brother, to the needy and to the poor, in your land.' "

The city of New York had a program for underprivileged kids called the "Fresh Air Fund," and the city would pay for a child to go stay with another family in another state, if the child's family qualified for the program. Eligibility was based on income, and Dad certainly qualified because he had such a large family to support. The program was "first come, first served" so that you had to get to the office on the first day of registration and sign up for the program.

The office was in the South Bronx, in a relatively rough neighborhood, and it opened on a Saturday morning at 9:00 a.m. Dad had Billy and me were there at 5:30 a.m. to make sure we were there early enough for registration.

Genesis 9:20 (NASB) … "Then Noah began farming and planted a vineyard."

The first year Billy and I were sent to Ohio to stay with a family that had a few boys and girls our age. We rode on a Greyhound bus for about eight hours and arrived having no idea where we were. Our "fresh-air" family met us at the bus station, and everyone seemed to get along fine for a while.

The program was for two weeks in the middle of the summer, and it was designed to keep us out of trouble at home. I guess the thinking was if we weren't home, we couldn't get into mischief!

The first day in Ohio was cool. We were on a farm, and that was quite different and exciting for us. In the morning, we woke up and went to the chicken coop to get eggs. We snatched them right out from under the chickens and brought them into the house to cook for breakfast. We were fired up about the newness in everything. In the afternoon, we went into the fields to pick beans and other vegetables.

Ezekiel 4:9 (ESV) ... "And you, take wheat and barley, beans and lentils, millet and emmer, and put them into a single vessel and make your bread from them. During the number of days that you lie on your side, 390 days, you shall eat it."

At first, the farm was intriguing until we realized we had to stay out in the hot field all day picking beans. Billy got frustrated because he figured we were being used as slave labor. He started battling with the Fresh Air family kids, and they became victims of his anger.

The father of the family was enraged with Billy and started to beat on him with the belt, and Billy's attitude was "I can get this at home," so he ran away. The police were called, and it turned into a serious matter. The family was petrified and didn't want to be reported or arrested for beating the poor needy Fresh Air Kids from the city, so they started to pamper me as if I was a king.

Needless to say, I cherished this new development, and secretly hoped Billy would hide out until it was time for us to head back to the Bronx. Billy went missing for an entire day, and they eventually found him sleeping in the smelly barn. After the father pledged not to discipline Billy and that we would no longer have to pick beans all day, Billy vowed not to run away again.

Being Catholic, we were instructed to never ever go into any church unless it was Catholic; otherwise, God would really be furious. This Fresh Air family was Protestant, and they tried to persuade us to go with them to church.

Billy declared, "Absolutely not!"

I, on the other hand, decided to give it a shot. From the minute I walked in I thought it was a big mistake. I sat in church, freaking out in my mind that I was going to burn in hell for such a grievous sin.

All was well for the duration of our stay, although Billy was never again part of the Fresh Air Fund. Regardless of what Billy did, I spent another few summers going to Pennsylvania to stay with a nice older couple who managed me just fine.

1 Peter 4:8 (NIV) … "Above all, love each other deeply, because love covers over a multitude of sins."

The Detwiler family, who was my next Fresh Air fund family, was a church-going, God-fearing older couple whose children had grown and moved away. Having me in their lives gave them some challenging moments coasting into those twilight years. The first time I got off the Greyhound bus in Pennsylvania, I watched as the other families gathered up the children assigned to them. As the crowd dwindled, I saw an older couple looking at one another in disappointment.

It wasn't long until we figured out that I was their Fresh Air kid. I was very distressed to hear that they had no children my age and not many kids in their neighborhood. Walking into the house I realized right away that the television was missing.

*Isaiah 41:13 (NLT) … "For I hold you by your right hand—I, the L*ORD *your God. And I say to you, 'Don't be afraid. I am here to help you.' "*

I asked Mrs. Detwiler where the television was, and she said, "We don't have one. We don't believe in wasting time watching TV."

For a moment, I just stood there in shock. My eyes became puffy, and I started to agonize. I felt as if I had been banished and sent to federal prison for two horrific weeks. I sat at the kitchen table while Mrs.Detwiler baked apple pies, and I wrote a painful letter to my dad saying it was a nightmare in Pennsylvania, and I anxiously wanted to get home.

Mrs. Detwiler became very concerned about my temperment, and when her husband got home from his errands, she made him go into the attic and yank down the tiny black and white television they had in storage.

Proverbs 17:17 (ESV) … "A friend loves at all times, and a brother is born for adversity."

I took possession of the television and put it smack in the middle of the kitchen table where it stayed until I left two weeks later. I asked Mrs. Detwiler about other children in the neighborhood, and she said there was a kid next door who was a little younger than me. "If you want to go over there, that will be fine."

Before the words were out of her mouth, I was over there banging on the neighbor's door. A woman with two young girls standing nearby answered the door, and I asked bluntly, "Is there a kid in the house I can play with?" Then I explained who I was and how I had come to stay in Pennsylvania.

They had a son named Greg, who at first was a little intimidated with my brash attitude. I assured him we could get along fine and that I wouldn't hurt him, and he finally came outside. He had a clubhouse in his backyard, and we hungout there most of the time.

Everything went well for the next two weeks with the Detwiler's taking me to church and with time spent at the clubhouse with Greg. I watched a lot of television shows at night like "The Twilight Zone" and "The Outer Limits," which were my favorites.

One day I went to the supermarket with Mrs. Detwiler and was amazed that the cigarettes were right out on the counter. Back home they were stashed behind the register, and you had to ask for them. I had picked up smoking back in the Bronx and thought it would be self-satisfying to enjoy a cigarette away from home. I had the impression everyone in this small town called "Downingtown" was as honest as could be because it was no sweat for me to rob a pack of cigarettes.

Once we arrived back to the Detwiler's house, I vanished into the garage that was a short distance from the house. As I ripped opened the pack of cigarettes, I realized they were non-filter cigarettes causing my arousal to deflate. I wasn't a five-star smoker when it came to non-filter cigarettes, but I went ahead and lit one up anyway. After a few puffs and coughing wildly, I decided I could wait until I got back to the Bronx for my next one.

The next day while we were sitting in the kitchen, Mrs. Detwiler asked, "Why do you smoke?"

I was stunned and speechless. After a few moments, I protested, "I don't smoke." I was forever freaked out by her question because after my protest, she never brought up the subject again.

Ephesians 6:18 (NASB) … "With all prayer and petition pray at all times in the Spirit, and with this in view, be on the alert with all perseverance and petition for all the saints."

I think that Mrs. and Mr. Detwiler prayed so hard and long for me over the years that their prayers were finally answered. I happily settled into their schedule and life and looked forward to going back every summer. I spent a good deal of my time trying to catch stray kittens that would come to the back door for food. I would position a milkbox held up with a stick, attach a rope to the stick, and when the kittens went under the lid, I could pull the rope, and conceivably, the box would fall down over them and entrap them. I must have tried a hundred times—with no luck. I started to believe my time and effort would be of no avail.

Each year, I would arrive at the Detwiler's house, and the first thing I would do is to scamper over to Greg's house to let him know I was back.

One year, as I bolted from the house after my arrival, Greg's two younger sisters were out on the curb in front of their house and I yelled out "Is Greg home?" In a playful and nonchalant manner in sequence, they responded, "NO, HE'S DEAD."

I shrugged off their response and continued to his front door. After ringing the doorbell several times, his mom came to the door, and I shouted, "Can Greg come out?"

His mom stood in stunned silence with tears rolling down her cheeks. I immediately thought back to what Greg's sisters had said on the curb "NO, HE'S DEAD."

I was invited into his house, and his mom asked me to have a seat on the couch. She then explained to me that Greg had become very sick from a disease known as "leukemia" and passed away only a few months earlier.

Stunned as I was, my first thought was that the only other kid in the neighborhood was living up the block, and before I had left the previous year, Greg and I made him our enemy. Now I had to convince this kid into believing our misunderstanding was all Greg's fault.

Proverbs 25:15 (ESV) ... "With patience a ruler may be persuaded, and a soft tongue will break a bone."

As I walked back into the Detwiler's house, Mrs. Detwiler was standing in the kitchen. She was totally speechless, and then slowly the words came out. "I'm so sorry, Johnny. I wanted to tell you just as you got off the bus, and it slipped my mind."

She sat me down, and I heard another version of what "leukemia" was while my mind drifted into what the next two weeks would look like.

I spent most of the day trying to catch the kittens with my milkbox trap with no success. On the day I had to go home, my scheme finally worked. I was in the kitchen with Mrs. Detwiler who was baking as always. The Detwilers had apple orchards, a field of corn, peach trees and every other kind of vegetable you could imagine—all right there on their property. Their basement was wall-to-wall jars of fruits and vegetables, cooked and canned and placed lovingly on shelves to store until they were needed for a pie or a meal.

On this final day of kitten trolling, I sat patiently behind the kitchen screen door waiting for the kittens to approach my trap. Three kittens were hiding in the bushes, looking longingly at the food until they could no longer resist the temptation. Finally, they sprinted toward the food and began to eat with gusto. I whispered, "Mrs. Detwiler, look! The kittens are under the box!" She stood and watched me as I was about to snatch-up the kittens.

Luke 12:30 (TLB) ... "All mankind scratches for its daily bread, but your heavenly Father knows your needs."

She said, "Johnny, God would not approve of your actions."

I just laughed and ignored her admonishment, excitedly waiting for the moment I would pull the rope. When the kittens were heads down in the food, I pulled the rope, and the milkbox trapped two of those little kitty bad boys inside. The third scampered back into the bushes.

I jumped up and down with passion, swinging my fist into the air and yelling, "I did it! I did it!" Mrs. Detwiler stood watching with a big smile on her face, knowing how long and hard I had tried to catch the kittens. She had told me that she didn't believe the kittens would fall for the trap, so she was doubly impressed with my achievement.

"I would like to sell the trophy kittens," I announced.

"I don't think that's a good idea," she answered.

"Well then, I'll just hang them by their necks on a tree and throw bricks at them!"

She knew I was being facetious, so she said, "Why not just let them go?"

I approached the milkbox and put my ear next to it, but I heard nothing. I thought I would open the box, and the kittens would romp and roll around in the grass and play with each other. In terror, when I lifted the box, both kittens came hurdling at me, wildly scratching at my face and neck.

Mrs. Detwiler had to run over and pull both wild creatures off me. I screamed in pain and anger, rubbing at the scratches on my face and neck. The little devils had nearly taken out my eyes, and I was badly shaken. I sat in the bathroom with Mrs. Detwiler caring for my wounds. I listened to her trying to hold in quiet giggles and trying to decide if I needed to go see the doctor.

She said in a serious whisper, "I told you God wouldn't approve of your actions."

I just started to laugh and said, "I'm glad my bus is leaving in a few hours."

Proverbs 28:1 (NLT) ... "The wicked run away when no one is chasing them, but the godly are as bold as lions."

The bus ride home was saturated with anticipation. Now that I had recovered from the assault by the kittens, I was looking forward to getting off the bus in New York to see Dad's expression when he saw my face full of scratches. He would really get a kick out of all the stories I had to tell.

Grand Central Station in New York City is a huge bus and train terminal, a cavernous, gigantic hall, with tens of thousands of people passing through daily. Yet, I wasn't intimidated! I knew Grand Central from when we would sneak on the trains at the Castle Hill Avenue station and journey down into the city.

I remember one frightening incident about Grand Central Station that stayed with me for life. Tommy T., Matthew, Billy and I had ventured off to a different state. I had gotten a bad report card and figured it would be better to run away from home than face Dad. So I asked Matthew and Billy if they wanted to run away with me.

"Sure," Billy replied.

"I'm not doing anything else today," Matthew said. "Sure why not?"

The three of us headed up to Tommy T.'s house to see if he also wanted to run away.

Matthew 5:42 (NIV) ... "Give to the one who asks you, and do not turn away from the one who wants to borrow from you."

Tommy T. answered the door when we knocked, and we asked him to step into the hallway. We squatted in the hallway for about thirty minutes after he agreed to run away with us, trying to decide where to go.

"I have a couple of hundred dollars I've saved," Tommy T. announced. "Want to go to Virginia? I'll pay for the bus ride!" He went back into the house to call the Greyhound bus company to find out the cost of the tickets.

Now pacing the hallway, Matthew, Billy and I couldn't wait to leave when Tommy T. came out and said we could take a bus to Washington, D.C., and walk over a short bridge to Virginia. The bus fare was $10.10 each, and we had to swear to pay Tommy T. back.

We made our solemn vow, and then hopped on the number 13 bus to the Castle Hill train station where we snuck on the train and headed down into Manhattan to Grand Central Station.

Exodus 23:9 (NASB) ... "You shall not oppress a stranger, since you yourselves know the feelings of a stranger, for you also were strangers in the land of Egypt."

We arrived at Grand Central around 6:00 p.m., purchased our bus tickets and were soon on our way to Washington, D.C. The bus ride was an adventure, and we fantasized about living the rest of our lives on the road. Tommy T. still had over a hundred dollars left, so we felt safe and secure. We arrived at the bus depot in Washington about 11:30 and eagerly jumped off the bus.

But we soon realized it wasn't all that exciting to be on our own, and a lot scarier than we had anticipated. It was as if we landed on another planet staring into the faces of cold expressionless, rag-torn homeless men who were staring right back at us like we were raw meat. We weren't sure where to go or where we would sleep that night. We were also hungry and scared no longer having envy for Washington. All of a sudden, we weren't so sure we even wanted to stay, considering the reality that had just set in.

Luke 15:18 (NIV) ... "I will set out and go back to my father and say to him: Father, I have sinned against heaven and against you."

Within minutes, Tommy T. had four tickets in his hand, and we took the same bus back to New York City. Now each of us owed Tommy T. $20.20 for a bus ride that had turned into nothing more than a round trip. We arrived back into Grand Central around 3:30 in the morning.

Grand Central Station at 3:30 a.m. was one of the spookiest places on earth, and a place we would rather have not been. We walked down very long, dark, creepy hallways, and our footsteps echoed in the quiet terminal. To make matters worse, we had noticed a shadowy figure of a man following us and hiding behind corners whenever we would look behind us.

Of course, our imaginations ran wild, and we spooked ourselves, becoming uneasy about this shadowy figure lurking in the dark corners. So we started to run, trying to escape from this mysterious man. The man hunted us all over Grand Central Station until we bolted into a corner to hide.

Joshua 1:9 (NIV) ... "Have I not commanded you? Be strong and courageous. Do not be afraid; do not be discouraged, for the LORD your God will be with you wherever you go."

Matthew started to laugh and said, "Why are we running?" We all agreed that we should face the bogey-man. But first we needed to be armed.

We saw a garbage can, and we found some bottles, broke off the bottoms to make our weapons of choice, and held the bottle necks with the sharp edges of glass protruding—perfect for stabbing and slashing.

The man approached us again without realizing we were now armed. He acted like a pervert; his manner and speech seemed to indicate that he had some fairly unpleasant plans for us. But when he caught a glimpse of our weapons, he broke and ran before his ceremonial bloodbath.

We were feeling pretty good now savoring our moment of victory, and all of a sudden, the early morning confines of Grand Central Terminal did not seem so threatening. We walked around until about 7:30 a.m. as the place started to come alive. Thousands of people were rushing to work, and we were determined to get something to eat.

Proverbs 6:31 (NIV) ... "Yet if he is caught, he must pay sevenfold, though it costs him all the wealth of his house."

We were just about to head into a small restaurant inside Grand Central when two men jumped out in front of us and yelled, "Operation Children"! They were holding out police badges in front of them; however, the men didn't look like any policemen we had ever seen.

Tommy T. was actually laughing at them, repeating their own words back at them. " 'Operation Children,' really?" But then he saw that they were serious.

Tommy T. and Billy took off running, while Matthew and I were taken into custody. We were marched into a room hidden from the public with a door that had been hidden behind a big billboard. The whole operation was all very secretive! The police explained that "Operation Children" was a police program established to catch runaways and kids playing hooky from school who would hang out at Grand Central Station.

They took all of our personal information, and they called my house first and then Matthew's house. My sister, Alice answered the phone and told them she was sending my brother, Tommy, downtown to pick me up. In the meantime, the officers tried to put a scare into us, so we would learn our lesson.

Matthew's Dad and my brother Tommy walked into the office at the same time. When we left, Matthew's dad slapped him in the head and curtly ordered, "Get home. I will deal with you later!"

Matthew took the train home with Tommy and me and endured his punishment for the offense. As for me, Tommy and Alice kept my confidence and never told Dad about the incident. I was one lucky kid!

John 16:32 (NIV) ... "A time is coming and in fact has come when you will be scattered, each to your own home. You will leave me all alone. Yet I am not alone, for my Father is with me."

My trip back from Pennsylvania and arrival into Grand Central Station seemed pretty explosive! I was excited to be back in the city. Commotion filled the air with sounds of trains and buses. My heart was racing. As we filed to the designated location where we would be rejoined with our family members, I watched as each family greeted their children with hugs and kisses. The crowd dwindled and dispersed, and still no one had come to claim me. A few people asked if I was alone, but I just answered, "My dad is in the bathroom." I finally walked away from the designated meeting spot. I didn't know what was happening, but I didn't want to make a scene.

Genesis 2:18 (ESV) ... "Then the Lord God said, 'It is not good that the man should be alone; I will make him a helper fit for him.' "

I got on the phone and called my house, but there was no answer. I didn't know whether I should wait to see if someone was coming to get me or take the train home. I waited for about an hour after everyone else had left. "Where could Dad be?"

Finally, I figured out that he was probably visiting his friend. I don't know if you would say my dad had a girlfriend, but with Mom in the hospital most of the time, he had taken a liking to another lady. She was also married, and her husband worked in the bar spending much of his time there. Given their mutual loneliness, Dad and his "lady friend" would often spend time together. She had three children, and Dad used to refer to her as a "close friend."

During these years, I guess I never gave a second thought, though I was not really sure of the nature of their relationship. He seemed to enjoy spending time with her, and I figured he deserved some company, so I was okay with it.

James 1:24 (NIV) ... "and, after looking at himself, goes away and immediately forgets what he looks like."

I called information on the pay phone and gave the operator her last name. The operator was able to get me the number. Her daughter answered, and I asked, "Is my dad there?" It was hard to hear what she said because it sounded as if there was a party going on.

Finally, Dad came to the phone and asked, "What do you want?"

When I told him where I was, he was shocked but laughed about the situation. "I thought you were coming home tomorrow. I'll send Tommy and Dorothy to pick you up."

Another hour or so went by, and my siblings finally showed up to rescue me. We had a good laugh about it after all was said and done. It turned out that his girlfriend's kid had a party, and Dad had a mental lapse. He just simply forgot I was coming home.

When I walked into our building after my two-week adventure in Pennsylvania, it was if I had never left. As usual, my friends were hanging out in the lobby. I told Dad I would be in the house shortly because I wanted to say hello to my friends, and he understood.

Isaiah 45:16 (NASB) ... "They will be put to shame and even humiliated, all of them; The manufacturers of idols will go away together in humiliation."

When you signed up with the Fresh Air Fund, you were given a name tag that said you were with that organization. It had a string you could use to hang the tag around your neck, so your host family would know they are picking up the right child. You also had to wear this name tag when you got off the bus at Grand Central Station to meet your family, though I'm not sure why. After all, I figured my family would recognize me when they saw me!

My usual routine was to take off the tag and put it in my pocket as soon as I could upon my return to Grand Central. As much as I might have enjoyed my time with the Detwilers, it was embarrassing to have people know that I was poor and was a part of the Fresh Air Fund program.

My friends didn't know about it because I always said I was going to sleep-away camp. This particular time, when no one was there to pick me up, I just put the name tag on the inside of my shirt, with the string still around my neck, and dismissed it from my mind.

Acts 17:5 (ESV) ... "But the Jews were jealous, and taking some wicked men of the rabble, they formed a mob, set the city in an uproar, and attacked the house of Jason, seeking to bring them out to the crowd."

As we plopped down on the lobby floor, I concocted stories of how I chased bears around the woods and made up other tales about my sleep-away adventures. That's when Gumby noticed the string around my neck. He lunged at me as I was talking and shouted, "What's this?" He pulled the string hard enough to choke me, but he didn't expose the name tag.

In a panic, I clutched his hand, and we went tumbling onto the lobby floor, wrestling each other for the string.

Now the gang was curious to know what I had in my shirt, and it turned into a "pile on" with about seven guys brawling in a tangle of bodies. Being as quick and flexible as I was, it allowed me to slip out of the pile and stand up and escape. I raced around the gigantic lobby columns and in and out the front doors of the building with everyone laughing and chasing me.

Acts 19:23 (NIV) … "About that time there arose no little disturbance concerning the Way."

The guys were maniacs now, and they were determined to find out what was under my shirt. I ran double-time toward my apartment with the gang in hot pursuit. I was praying that the door would be unlocked. As I reached the door and turned the knob, I felt it catch in my hand, and my heart sank. The door was locked! The clock had run out on my escape. A pile of young boys descended, with every-one grabbing at my neck.

I was holding on to the door knob for dear life, pushing up against the door, and hunching into a crouched position, to keep them from digging into my shirt. A bundle of thrashing arms and legs punched, kicked and screamed outside my apartment door, and just as Tommy T. was about to pry my hand loose, the door opened.

We all fell as one into my apartment and looked up to find my dad standing over us.

He was obviously angry, and he shouted, "What is going on?"

There was a slight pause, and then everyone took off running. I tried to run too, but Dad pulled me inside and asked again, "What's going on?"

"Umm, my friends were welcoming me home from my vacation."

I ran into the bathroom and bolted the door behind me, my heart pounding in my chest. I pulled the name tag from my neck, ripped it into a hundred pieces, flushed it down the toilet, and out of sight. I silently vowed that the next time I went to Pennsylvania I would destroy the tag the minute I got off the bus!

SAY GOODBYE TO THE 60S

▲ ▲ ▲

PHILIPPIANS 3:14 (NIV) … "I press on toward the goal to win the prize for which God has called me heavenward in Christ Jesus."

Graduating from the sixth grade could have been an eye-popping event in my life. At the end of each school year, you would receive a report card, which would tell you whether you would be promoted to the next grade or "left back" or repeat a grade. I always had to sweat it out, never knowing which way it would go for me. When we were about to graduate from sixth grade, I did catch wind that I was getting promoted and couldn't wait for graduation.

Graduation was the most exciting event that had ever happened to me, especially since this year would be the first time I'd get announced on the stage to receive an award. If you were a member of the AAA squad of guards, you automatically received an award, but that didn't diminish the exhilarating dignity I was sensing. I asked Gumby if he wanted to come to the luncheonette for some Jelly doughnuts—as my treat. In my justifiable pride and zeal over the impending award ceremony, I was feeling particularly in a giving mood. Of course, Gumby took full advantage at my offer.

1 Peter 3:4 (NIV) ... "Rather, it should be that of your inner self, the unfading beauty of a gentle and quiet spirit, which is of great worth in God's sight."

The luncheonette had prizewinning jelly doughnuts, and that day I decided I would have a double portion. Halfway through the second doughnut, I started to feel weird. I put down the doughnut and stared off into space, turning my attention inward and trying to get a grip on what was going on inside my body.

"What's wrong?" Gumby asked.

I couldn't explain how I felt. I said that I needed to get home. As we were leaving the luncheonette, Gumby bolted back to where I had been sitting and grabbed the rest of my doughnut, declaring loudly that my estimate of the jelly doughnut quality was right on the money.

James 5:14 (ESV) ... "Is anyone among you sick? Let him call for the elders of the church, and let them pray over him, anointing him with oil in the name of the Lord."

By the time I walked in my house, I was sweating like a pig, and I had a high fever. The doctor came to our apartment to examine me, and he said I had something called the "Hong Kong flu." I had never been to Hong Kong, and I wasn't even sure that I knew where it was, so I didn't understand how I could have the Hong Kong flu. But I did!

I got sicker and sicker, and as my fever rose, I started to hallucinate. I saw myself at my sixth grade graduation, receiving my distinctive award and being pushed on to the seventh grade. I saw everyone in the crowd screaming and applauding as I walked up on the stage. It was definitely the best day in my life!

Grievously, the best day of my life would remain a dream I could not fulfill. I had such a bad case of the flu, I was in bed for two weeks, and I missed my graduation and the honor of standing on the stage to receive my long-awaited award. I also missed the last day of school! I tried to comfort myself recollecting my confirmation ceremony the year before and how significant that event had been.

Isaiah 63:2 (NASB) … "Why is Your apparel red, And Your garments like the one who treads in the wine press?"

Everyone wore long, bright-red gowns for confirmation. As a gag, a few guys sported nothing underneath the gowns, and we spent the day pulling up gowns to see who was bare and who was wearing underwear.

Dad took me to the Boulevard Bar that day as a gift, and with my special "stand-out-in-a-crowd" gear, most of the drunks at the bar gave me money in honor of my special day. Only one intoxicated fool found my bright-red gown somewhat distracting, and he screeched at me for taking his mind off his pool game.

Dad almost took the guy's head off for spoiling my day, and then asked me to have a seat and try not to distract anyone else or make trouble.

Psalm 121:7 (NIV) … "The LORD will keep you from all harm—he will watch over your life."

I was watching the television in the bar, trying to mind my own business so everyone would forget I was there. I knew I stuck out like a sore thumb in my red gown—even though I was pretty proud of my achievement, and I didn't want to take it off.

As I stared at the grainy television screen, I found myself thinking about Robert Kennedy, though I don't know why. I thought about how he had recently been assassinated and about how his brother, our President, had not even been safe from the hatred and violence. I suppose I felt that, by virtue of my confirmation, I had taken a step toward manhood, and I was beginning to understand how the world worked.

Sitting in the bar that day, trying to fit in with a group of adults as they attempted to escape from the woes of the world, I got the perception that in the grownup world, if you didn't like someone you might just be inclined to shoot them. Immediately, I hunkered down on the bar stool and tried to make myself as small and inconspicuous as possible. With my newfound knowledge of grownup conflict came the recognition that I might have to learn how to avoid being shot!

ONE SMALL STEP FOR MAN

▲ ▲ ▲

REVELATION 22:13 (AKJV) ... I am Alpha and Omega, the beginning and the end, the first and the last.

As I continued my education in life, I got a little older every day. The hot summers came and went as did the cold winters, passing more quickly now, and soon the decade of the 1960s would be over.

One day, Dad called me out of my room and told me to come into his bedroom. "Johnny, go and round up the family. Tell them to get home within the next thirty minutes or else they would be in a lot of trouble."

I could see he wasn't kidding! He had to make sure we saw something important. I ran to the park where I knew my brothers would be hanging out, and I told them to get home fast. Then I ran back home and headed upstairs to where I knew Dorothy would be, and I told her to go home.

We all gathered in Dad's bedroom, where he was lying on the bed, and he announced that history was about to be made. "You're all going to be witnesses." Standing around the television, we watched as Neil Armstrong stepped onto the moon's surface and spoke these now-famous words: "That's one small step for man, one giant leap for mankind." I watched in awe and thought about my own future.

Luke 1:30 (ESV) … "And the angel said to her, 'Do not be afraid, Mary, for you have found favor with God.' "

With a new decade coming and my own giant step into adolescence, I wondered how the 1970s would turn out. I wondered if there would be another war and if any other leaders would be killed. What about the 1980s and the 1990s, which seemed impossibly distant and unimaginable?

I didn't know it then, but within a few short years, we would move out of the projects. Shortly thereafter, my mother would commit suicide, and our good friend, Gumby would almost die from a severe drug overdose! On that day, as I watched Neil Armstrong walking on the moon, I found it hard to believe that the 60s were coming to an end.

WELCOME TO MY LIFE!

▲ ▲ ▲

2 CORINTHIANS 5:17 (KJV) … "Therefore if any man be in Christ, he is a new creature: old things are passed away; behold, all things are become new."

On New Year's Eve in 1969, we sat watching Guy Lombardo count down to midnight, and as the ball dropped in Times Square, we said goodbye to a decade—the 1960s—the only one I could clearly remember. In spite of my feelings of confusion and anxiety, in spite of the fact that I had no idea what the future would hold, I found myself excited.

I did not know that I would go on to be married to a wonderful woman, and we would have three unbelieveably gifted God fearing children. I didn't know and would never have imagined that I would someday live happily in another state. Yet, somehow on that New Year's Eve, as we welcomed in the 70s, I could now think about my future and my past, as I knew things would be okay. It really didn't matter to me what the future held! I found it exciting just to be alive and to face the new decade.

The 1970s would be an adventure, and by the time that decade ended, I would be an adult! I could not wait for my life to start! I never dreamed or thought I would actually write a book entitled

"*God Verses the Bad Boy*," and most of all, that such awesome people would actually pick it up and read it. With all my heartfelt passion, I want to thank everyone who took precious time from their busy lives to read this book, and most of all my hope is that the Scriptures in this book have accomplished what the good Lord had intended.

MARIE'S FAVORITES

▲ ▲ ▲

Proverbs 31:10 (ESV) ... *"An excellent wife who can find? She is far more precious than jewels."*

My beautiful wife Marie has her favorite stories about my childhood that I forgot about, and she insisted that I include them. So the following are two of Marie's favorites:

Genesis 3:10 (ESV) ... *"And he said, 'I heard the sound of you in the garden, and I was afraid, because I was naked, and I hid myself.' "*

As young children, we would play hide and seek in the house as a great escape from boredom. One day, as we were playing, I decided to hide in one of my favorite spots—inside the bathroom clothes hamper. Skinny and small in build, I was able to crawl into the hamper and dig my way to the bottom. I would cover myself with the dirty smelly clothes and lie there until my brother or sister would give up. Then, I would come out of hiding.

One day hiding in my favorite spot someone opened the bathroom door, and then I heard the door lock. I heard the shower turned on and the water running. Someone then opened the hamper cover and dropped more clothes on top of the pile covering me. As I made my way through the clothes to the top, I peeked out of the hamper.

I could have died right there and then. Mom was standing there naked as a jaybird! I sank back down to the bottom of the hamper as nervous as ever. I could hear my brother calling for me to come out from hiding. I just ignored him while I tried to figure out how to get out of there without getting caught.

When Mom stepped into the shower, I slowly and quietly opened the lid of the hamper, jumped out, grabbed the bathroom door, and got out as quickly as I could. My heart was still pumping as I heard Mom yell out, "Who's there?"

I told Billy what had happened, and we laughed about it all day— although I couldn't look at Mom for a few days without turning red.

1 Thessalonians 5:2 (ESV)… "For you yourselves are fully aware that the day of the Lord will come like a thief in the night."

When things got tight around our house, and we didn't have enough money for some kind of evening snack, we would just do without. Well, *we kids* did without but not Dad, who always had his personal stash of cupcakes in the cabinet for his evening snack around 9:00 p.m.

Feeling hungry one evening, I decided to steal dad's cupcakes around 8 p.m. I quietly tiptoed into the kitchen and lifted the cupcakes into my shirt and walked to the bathroom. Once in the bathroom, I ripped the pack open and ate the two cupcakes as fast as I could with the hope that no one had to use the bathroom.

After a few times, Dad caught on to what I was doing, but he stayed silent about the matter. Meanwhile, I was feasting on Dad's cupcakes every night. Dad knew how to catch me, and his plan worked really well.

I woke up one morning, and my whole bed seemed to be filled with the "aftermath" of diarrhea. Not feeling very well, I went crying to Dad that something was seriously wrong with me.

"Step over here," he answered.

I thought he would feel my head to determine whether or not I had a fever. Instead, once I got close enough, he hit me so hard I went flying across the room. As I got up in shock to ask why he had hit me, he shouted, "Why did you steal the cupcakes?"

When I didn't answer, he explained that he had slipped some ex-lax® into the cupcakes, and that was the reason for my bed and body being a mess. I then received a lecture on the purpose of ex-lax®, which was designed to cleanse the body of human waste.

I learned the product came in the form of a small chocolate wafer so I couldn't tell the difference between it and the cupcakes.

I learned my lesson soundly. That was the last time I ever stole anything pertaining to Dad's food or snacks!

JOHNNY'S TAKEAWAY

▲ ▲ ▲

REVELATION 22:19 (NIV) ... "AND if anyone takes words away from this scroll of prophecy, God will take away from that person any share in the tree of life and in the Holy City, which are described in this scroll."

My conclusion is that "Bad-Boy" Johnny was living a double life. He lived one life pre-Genesis 3:6. The other life he lived post-Genesis 3:6 (ESV), which says, *"So when the woman saw that the tree was good for food, and that it was a delight to the eyes, and that the tree was to be desired to make one wise, she took of its fruit and ate, and she also gave some to her husband who was with her, and he ate."*

At times Johnny solely depended upon God as in pre-Genesis 3:6, while other times he depended upon himself as in post-Genesis 3:6.

As an adult, Johnny tries very hard to live pre-Genesis 3:6, but fails most often. Johnny has found that reading Scripture daily helps him stay grounded in pre-Genesis 3:6.

The more than 260 verses of Scripture squeezed Johnny so tightly. it condensed his life into one single verse of scripture which is as follows:

"For God so loved the world that he gave his one and only Son, that whoever believes in him shall not perish but have eternal life" (John 3:16, NIV).

WITH GRATITUDE

▲ ▲ ▲

Proverbs 3:6 (NKJV) … "In all your ways acknowledge Him, And He shall direct your paths."

Very special thanks to **Jim Heldt** who took the time to patiently listen to me as I tried to explain my vision for the image on the front cover of this book. His magnificent talent in drawing and painting produced the wonderful cover for "God Verses The Bad Boy", and it has surpassed all of my expectations.

The "Fresh Air Fund" is still in existence today, and I sincerely hope anyone looking to support a great organization will "Google" the name.

Some of the amazing folks who injected some inspiration, thought, hard work or effort into "God Verses The Bad Boy" include the following:

Ken Adams	Larry Bartram
Mike Adkins	Bill Behr
Sam Arocho	Renee & Josh Cartlidge
Jon Aron	Britton Cox

Isaiah Dennis

Dave Duncan

Stephanie M. Grossman

David Guarino

Bill Harrington

Darling & Brian Heldt

Brian Hogan

Isaac Hunter

Amanda Kossina

Lauren Lanker

Tracey Leath

Mark Lorentz

Donna Mantlo

Sherry Mosher

Faith Murray

Marie Murray

Michael Murray

Thomas Murray

Kailey Newkirk

Amanda Ober

Tina Therrien-O'Brien

Vincent Orlando

John Parker

Terrance Jerome Rogers

Joe Saviano

Margaret Saviano

Rich Sementa

Laura Shriver

Matt Spikes

Zach Van Dyke

FINANCIAL CONTRIBUTORS

▲ ▲ ▲

Ron Jon Allegro

Jon Aron

Julie and Manny Banzon

Dustin Berger

Gary Bolton

Kristen Chandler

John & Angie Crossman

Lynda Boggia-Duncan

Sasha Griffith

Darling & Brian Heldt

Jeff Herman

Chace Hulon

Margaret M. Kaylor

Dr. Brenda Kelly

Michael & Diana Murray

Faith Murray

Rinaldo and Enid Perciballi

Barbara Savidge

Laura Shriver

Proverbs 3:5 (NIV) ... Trust in the Lord with all your heart and lean not on your own understanding;

If you'd like to contact the Bad Boy with Questions or comments, please visit his website ... www.Godversesthebadboy.com